Museum of
Mosaic and Frescoes
M Chora

Museum of Chora

Mosaic and Frescoes

Archaeologist

İlhan Akşit

akşit

AKŞIT KÜLTÜR VE TURİZM YAYINCILIK

Edited by

AKŞİT KÜLTÜR ve TURİZM YAYINCILIK

■ ■ ■

Written by

İlhan Akşit

■ ■ ■

Translated by

Ayşenaz - Kubilay Koş

■ ■ ■

Graphic Composition

Zafer Emecan

■ ■ ■

Typesetting

Gülcan Lazım

■ ■ ■

Correction

Ali Kılıçkaya

■ ■ ■

Photos

Tahsin Aydoğmuş

Vasken Değirmentaş

Kadir Kır

Erdal Yazıcı

Güngör Özsoy

■ ■ ■

Colour Separation

Figür Grafik

■ ■ ■

Printed by

Ohan Matbaacılık Ltd.Şti.

Hadımköy Yolu Çakmaklı Mah. San 1 Bulvarı

4. Bölge 9. Cd. No:143 Çakmaklı-B.Çekmece/ISTANBUL

Tel : (+90 212) 886 70 70

■ ■ ■

Akşit Kültür ve Turizm Yayıncılık

Cağaloğlu Yokuşu Cemal Nadir Sokak

Nur İş Hanı 2/4 Cağaloğlu

34440-ISTANBUL / TURKEY

Tel : (+90 212) 511 53 85 – 511 67 82

Fax: (+90 212) 527 68 13

Internet: www.aksityayincilik.com

e-mail: aksit@aksityayincilik.com

■ ■ ■

Contents

Preface

The church of the monastery of Chora, situated in the Edirnekapı quarter of Istanbul today, was re-erected by the Emperor Justinianos on the site of an ancient chapel within the premises of a monastery. The monastery was named as 'chora' meaning a land outside of the city walls, but had continued to be referred to as 'chora' even after the borders of the city had been expanded beyond it.

Having reached to the Komnenos era with some repairs and restorations, it suffered the same fate of the city's other churches during the Latin invasion and was in ruins. However, after the invasion, it was restored by Theodor Metochites who was an important figure of his time, and it was decorated with mosaics that arouse in the beholder a deep sense of admiration even today.

Metochites who dedicated himself to the restoration of this monastery and church, and who adorned the church with unique mosaics, had a cemetery chapel erected there, as well. This chapel was also adorned with mosaics and frescoes by himself. Although Metochites successfully attained important roles in the political and social life of his period, he fell into disfavor upon the downfall of the emperor and was sent into exile. Later on, when he was pardoned and permitted to return to Istanbul, he was installed in his beloved monastery and lived there as a destitute monk until his death. We have given a particular attention to Theodor Metochites and to his turbulent life in this book, taking into consideration his integral role in the worldwide fame of the Chora Monastery thanks to the decorations made between the years 1303 and 1320.

In order for the visitor of the Chora Museum to easily follow the mosaics and frescoes, we have assigned them numbers, starting from the left side of the nartex, without considering the chronological order, and included them all in our book. Moreover, we have put the theme of each mosaic next to its picture. Thus, the mosaics and their stories have attained an integrity for the reader.

In our book, we have tried to present to you the unique mosaics and frescoes of this church which perfectly reflects the Palaiologos era of the Byzantine Art. Now, we leave you alone with these magnificient mosaics and their mysterious world.

Respectfully,
Ilhan Akşit

*P*lan of the *C*hora *M*useum

A   1. Jjourney to Bethlehem

2. Holy family's journey to Jerusalem

3. Medallions of the saints

4. Christ among the doctors

5. John the Baptist bearing witness of Christ

6. The census count

7. Medallions of the saints

A-B 8. Anne and Mary

9. St. Andronicus

10. Other saints

11. Tarachus

12. St. Joachim

Tomb G (15th century)

B   13. Return of the Holy Family from
Egypt to Nazareth

14. Medallions of the saints (St. Laurus, St.
Flarus, St. Menas of Phrygia, St. Victor, St. Vincentus)

15. Jesus' baptism by John the Baptist

16. Temptation of Christ

17. Birth of Christ

18. Medallions of the saints (St. Philemon, St.
Leucius, St. Agathanicus, St. Thyrsus, St. Appollonius)

B-C 19. Mary and Christ Child

20. St. George

21. An unidentified saint

C   22. The Virgin Blachernitissa above the entrance door

23. Christ Pantocrator above the entrance
to the inner narthex

24. The Cana miracle (water being turned to wine)

25. Multiplication of the loaves

C-D 26. John the Baptist

27. St. Demetrius

28. An unidentified saint

Tomb F (dated 1330, tomb of a member of a Palaiologos family)

D   29. Flight of Elizabeth and John the Baptist

30. St. Eugraphus, Menas of Alexandria, Hermogenes

31. An unidentified scene

32. Christ healing a leper

33. St. Abius, St. Gurias, St. Samonas

34. The Magi before Herod

D-E 35. An unidentified saint

36. An unidentified saint

37. An unidentified soldier saint

Tomb E Tomb of Irene Raulaina Palaiologos 1325

E   38. St. Sergius or St. Bacchus

39. Mothers' mourning

40. Interrogation of King Herod

41. An unidentified saint

F   42. The Samaritan woman at the well

43. Massacre of the innocent

44. Command for killing of the innocent

45. Christ healing a blind man

46. Healing of a paralytic in Bethseida Pool

47. Healing of a paralytic in Capernaum

F-K 48. St. Euthymius

K   49. Holy Family's flight to Egypt

50. Magi returning to the East

51. An unidentified scene

J   52. An unidentified scene

53. Christ healing a man with the withered hand

54. Christ healing a leper

55. Christ Pantocrator and the ancestors

56. Christ's genealogy 1st Line

57. Christ's genealogy 2nd Line

58. Christ healing a blind and dumb man

59. Christ healing the multitude

60-62-64-67. Medallions of angels

61. Christ healing two blind men

63. Christ healing Peter's mother-in-law

65. Christ of Chalke and Virgin Mary

66. Christ healing the woman with the issue of blood

J-I 68. St. Paul

69. The Virgin fed by an angel

70. Education of the Virgin in the temple

I   71. The Virgin receiving the skein of wool for the temple

72. Presentation of the Virgin to the temple

73. Metochites presenting the model of the
church to Jesus

I-H 74. St. Peter

75. First seven steps of Mary

76. Zachariah praying for the rods of the suitors

H   77. Mary's engagement with Joseph

78. Mary's blessing by the priests

79. Mary caressed by her parents

80. Birth of the Virgin

H-G 81. Joachim and Anne meeting at the Golden Gate

82. Joseph taking the Virgin to his House

G   83. Genealogy of Mary

84. Medallions of angels

85. Joseph taking leave of Mary

Tomb H the Tomb of despot Demetrius Palaiologos
who died in 1340

86. Joachim's offering rejected

87. Annunciation to St. Anne

88. Joachim in wilderness

89. A medallion of an angel

90. Annunciation to Mary at the well

91. Death of the Virgin

92. Christ

93. The Virgin Hodegetria

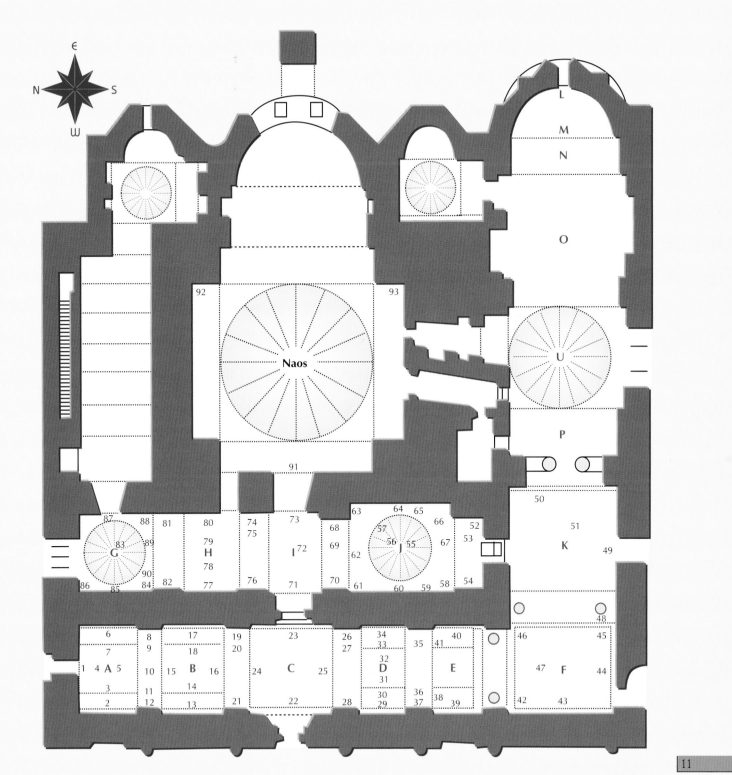

Chora (Kariye) Museum

Situated in the Edirnekapı quarter of Istanbul, the Chora Museum famous for its adorable mosaics takes its name from the Greek word 'chora', refering to a land outside of the city or village. The Monastery of Chora was named as such, because it was lay outside the city walls built by the Emperor Constantine. Although the monastery lay within the city walls that were later built by the Emperor Theodosius in 423 A.D., its name remained unchanged. During the reign of the Emperor Justinianos, the monastery was devastated by an earthquake on October 6, 557. The Emperor had then rebuilt the monastery in the form of a basilica. The monastery was again in ruins in the 8th century and it was restored in 843 A.D. After that date, there is a complete lack of information concerning the history of the Chora Monastery until the 12th century. During the Komnenos dynasty, the monastery was again in a heap of ruins. We know that it was restored and rebuilt by Maria Dukaena, the mother-in-law of the Emperor Alexios I Komnenos (1081-1118). Isaakios Komnenos (1185-1195), the third son of Alexios Komnenos who was the grandson of Maria Dukaena, had also taken part in the restoration, and hence he was depicted next to the Virgin in the panel of Jesus Christ and Virgin Mary.

Although all the churches in Istanbul were devastated during the 57 year-long occupation of the city by the Latins from 1204 till 1261, this church was not destroyed. The monastery taken by the Orthodox Priests, was later again in ruins due to negligence in maintenance. Meanwhile, the Byzantine Emperor Mikhail Palaiologos VIII (1259-1282)

An aerial view of Kariye Museum

A view from southeastern front

who had formed a government in Nicaea, tried to repair and restore the ruined churches, together with other prominent state authorities, after returning to Istanbul.

Later on, the monastery was successfully restored by Theodore Metochites, being the controller of the treasury during the reign of Andronikos II (1282-1328), and residing nearby the monastery. He was a poet and a man of letters as well. Since the turbulent life of Metochites will be covered in detail in the following chapters, it is better to continue now with the history of the monastery.

After the conquest of Istanbul by the Turks in 1453, the Chora Monastery was converted into a mosque in 1511 by Atik Ali Pasha, the grand vizier of Sultan Bayezit II. No amendment was made to its architecture except the addition of a minaret; however, the name of the Chora Monastery became Kariye, and it was known as the Kariye Mosque since then. After the conquest, the mosaics of the church which had been converted to a mosque were not touched. During the restoration in 1765, although there were small architectural additions, the mosaics were protected as they were. However, these mosaics were covered by wooden curtains during the daily prayers, as it is forbidden to pray in Islam in the presence of any form of picture.

The famous Turkish explorer Evliya Celebi who lived in the 17th century had visited the monastery and mentioned its mosaics in his writings. Furthermore, in 1822 Hammer published a catalogue of the mosaics. From all these facts,

Detail of the scene of 'the Virgin's presentation to the temple', in the inner narthex

Detail showing the priest in the scene of 'blessing of the Virgin'

we can understand that even though the church of Chora had been converted into a mosque, its mosaics were note scraped or erased by the Turks, but kept as they were.

The Chora was sometimes opened to visitors in the Ottoman period. The most important visitor was the German Emperor Willhem II who visited Istanbul in the 1890s.

After the conversion of the mosque into a museum, the American Byzantine Institute repaired it from 1948 till 1958. The plasters and the paint covering the mosaics and frescoes were removed and cleaned, and the decorations have acquired the recent appearance after the restoration work.

Architecture and Adornments

To the present day, only the church has remained of the Chora Monastery complex. As the building consisted of a naos and a narthex in its initial construction, the main structure was kept intact after the repairs and additions; only an annex was made to the north of the structure and an outer narthex to the west. In addition, a long and narrow chapel called Paracclesion, was added to the south. This single-naved, long and narrow chapel covered with a dome was constructed over the cellar. The east wing ends with an apse. All the round arches, semi-supports, niches, as well as the brick-laying workmanship on the façades of the building add a sense of movement to the outer look and save the building from being perceived as a massive block. The present building covers an area of 27.5 meters by 27 meters, The length of the Parecclesion is 29 meters. The church has six domes the greatest of which is situated in the center with a diameter of 7.70 meters. Two domes are located in the inner narthex, and the other two are on the right and left sides of the apse. The second greatest dome after the central one is located in the Parecclesion with a diameter of 4.50 meters. The apse has three windows. The inner walls of the main building are covered with marbles of wonderful colors. The inner narthex is of 4 meter width and of 18 meter length. There is a door here, leading to the Parecclesion. The outer narthex on the other hand is of 4

The scene of 'the first seven steps of Mary' in the inner narthex, No. 75

meter width and 23.30 meter length. The niches in the outer narthex and in the annexed chapel had been used as tombs.

The mosaics were made by drawing draft pictures on a fast drying plaster and then sticking colored pieces of stones, bricks and glass over them. As gold was also used in the mosaics during the reign of the Emperor Justinian, magnificent pieces of art were created. In the 14th century, during the Palaiologos dynasty, the art of mosaic ornamentation had shown a big development. The Chora Monastery built in this period is the most significant evidence of that. The works of mosaic and fresco ornamentation in the church were started in 1303 and completed in 1320. In order to create a three-dimension effect in the compositions, scenes with landscapes, houses and mountains were used in the background, and depictions were made realistic. The figures keeping their feet on the ground, were placed according to perspective rules. Empty spaces were furnished with details of the theme, and figures of tree and house. There are also inscriptions on the mosaics explaining the scene. Hues of blue, green and red are used harmoniously in the figures. The background is goldgilt.

As it can be seen in the depictions of the saints and garments of Theodoros Metochites, the vestments reflect the magnificence of the palace. The themes taken up in the inner and outer narthexes follow each other periodically just like the serial sequences of a comic book. In the north wing of the inner narthex, eighteen incidents concerning the life cycle of the Virgin are depicted with all its beauty. Those on the north side of the outer narthex describe the important events in the life of the holy family as well as the birth of Christ and his baptism, whereas the miracles of Jesus and his other deeds while spreading the word of God can be found in the south wings of both narthexes.

However, because of the falling of the plasters, many of the important mosaics have not survived to the present day. The short inscriptions on the mosaics are text or symbols explaining that particular mosaic. The mosaics made

The mosaic of 'Christ of the Chalke' and the Virgin in the inner narthex No. 65

On the next pages: 'Genealogy of Mary' in the northern dome of the inner narthex

naturally with a harmonious blend of colors arouse a deep sense of admiration in the beholder.

All of the scenes in the mosaics of the church contain subjects from the Old and New Testaments and reflect the life cycles of Mary and Jesus. In our book, we see it easier to start the tour of the museum from the left side of the

Depiction of Jesus with the Bible in his hand in the north side of the apse in the main bay of the museum

Figures of Jesus and Mary at each side of the apse

entrance door, without following the chronological order, and to see the mosaics in the outer narthex one by one, by following the numbers in the plan we have provided, and then conclude our tour through the inner narthex and the main bay, at the annexed chapel. But before starting to trace them according to the plan, let us here explain the themes of the mosaic panels in brief, in chronological order. Thus we will be able to provide a section for the visitors who would like to trace them in their chronologic cycles.

There was a priest named Zachariah in the days of Herod I, the king of Judaea. He and his wife Elizabeth had no child; Zachariah was deeply sad for this. Gabriel one day visited him while he was praying in the temple, to give him the good news that he would have a child, and told him to call him John. Finally Elizabeth gave birth to a boy named John.

John grew up. It was the reign of the Roman Emperor Tiberius, and Herod Antipas was the king of Galilee. God had spoken to John in the desert. And John walked all around the Jordan River preaching the baptism of repentance for the remission of sins. All the people of Judaea and Jerusalem were baptized with the waters of Jordan River. And, as the people were in expectation, they asked him if he was a 'Messiah' or not. John answered them saying "I indeed baptize you with water; but one mightier than I will come and will baptize you with the Holy Ghost and with fire." Thus, John was announcing the coming of the Christ.

Herod Antipas nursing a grudge against John, imprisoned him and had him killed on the pretext of recent events.

Joachim and Anne were both of the lineage of David, and had no child. On a feast day, when Joachim went to the temple to make a sacrifice, he was driven away by the priest since he had no child. Joachim who was deeply

saddened, ascended up into the mountains and passed his days with shepherds. He stayed up there praying for 40 consecutive days and nights. Finally, Gabriel visited Anne to give her the news that she would be expecting a child and meeting her husband at the Golden Gate of Jerusalem. Anne greeted her husband at the Golden Gate as Gabriel had foretold and this elderly couple later had a girl named Mary. The mosaics concerning this story and first seven steps of Mary can be seen in the inner narthex of the Chora Monastery.

Since her family had promised to leave their child in a temple if they had one, they kept their promise and left Mary in the care of a temple when she was 3-5 years old.

Relief of Jesus among marble adornments above the Virgin figure in the main bay

She stayed in the temple for 12 years and when she was 14-15 years old, the priests told her that she was old enough to get married. However, Mary told them that she devoted herself to God. At this time, the Head Priest Zachariah saying that he had a revelation from an angel, called all the suitors together and placed their rods on the altar. He told that Mary would be entrusted to the one whose rod turns to green. They all gathered at the temple one night. When morning came, the rod of Joseph, a carpenter from Nazareth, began to sprout green leaves and the Virgin Mary was awarded to him.

One day Gabriel visited Joseph's fiancé in Galilee and broke the news that she would conceive and bring forth a son

from God and she should name her newborn child as Jesus.(Luke 1: 26-37) Gabriel also told her that her cousin Elizabeth had also conceived a son in her old age and that with God nothing would be impossible. Mary went to visit her cousin Elizabeth in order to see whether or not what the angel had said was true. She remained there for 3 months until John was born. When she returned, Joseph found it hard to believe her story of the visit from the angel. However, an angel appeared to him as well in a dream. "Joseph, son of David," the angel said, "Fear not to take Mary as your wife, for that which is conceived in her is of

the Holy Ghost. She shall bring forth a son and you shall call him Jesus, for he shall save the people from their sins." No longer doubting then, Joseph guarded the young mother and her precious gift against the spiteful tongues of those who would not believe that. The year in which these events happened, Caesar Augustus, the Emperor of Rome, had decreed that a census count be made in all of the Roman provinces. And since everyone was required to return to the city of his birth, Joseph and Mary traveled to Bethlehem from Nazareth to register for the census. Census count was made during the reign of the King Cyrenius of Syria. Jesus

The scene of 'the death of the Virgin' above the entrance to the main bay (naos)

was born in Bethlehem. In the scene that shows the birth of Jesus, Mary, Joseph and baby Jesus are depicted in a stable in Bethlehem. Angels gave the good news to the shepherds abiding in the fields and the shepherd then visited Jesus in swaddling clothes, lying in a manger.

At the time Jesus was born, King Herod had three stranger visitors who one day appeared in Jerusalem. For they identified themselves as wise men or Magi, they asked him the question which had brought them there: "Where is he that is born King of the Jews? We have come to worship him." The king then ordered them to go and find that child and bring him word where the child might be found so that he could worship it. The three Magi found Mary and the infant Jesus, and they worshipped the newborn baby. But being warned by God in a dream that they should not go back to Herod, they left for their own country by another route. The arrival of the Magi along with a big caravan is called "the Journey of the Magi Kings", and their worshipping to Jesus is described as "kings worshipping before the infant Jesus". One of these Magi was young, one was middle-aged and one was old. Their names were Melkior, Baltazar and Gaspar. When the Magi did not return, Herod resorted to one of the most brutal acts in history, in order to destroy the Messiah. He decreed that all children under the age of two in Bethlehem and its environs be executed. The mosaics showing Herod giving the order for the deaths of innocent people and the application of this order can be seen in the south wing of

Mosaic of Jesus' Genealogy in the dome and Deesis Mosaic below
A view from the inner narthex

the outer narthex. Joseph and Mary were troubled by the knowledge that Herod had learned Jesus' birth. And Joseph was warned in a dream that they should flee into Egypt where the king could not harm them. Unfortunately, the mosaics depicting the Holy Family's journey to Egypt have not survived to the present day. When the word of Herod's death was brought by an angel to Joseph in Egypt, he decided to return to their homeland, but did not stop at Bethlehem since it was near to Jerusalem. Instead, they continued on to Nazareth. Meantime, Archelaus, son of Herod, also called Herod became the ruler of Judeae. Jesus was baptized by John when he was 30 years old. The subject of Satan tempting Jesus can be seen on a big panel. The miracles of Jesus are depicted in the southern wing and at four sides of the mosaic of Jesus in the dome. The scenes of turning water into wine and multiplication of bread are found in the outer narthex whereas a number of miracles such as blind and mute souls being healed are depicted in the other parts. Furthermore, one can see the Chalke mosaic and the mosaic of Theodore Metochites as he gives Jesus a model of the church.

The scene of Mary's death 'Koimesis' is found on the inside of the gate that passes into the naos of the church. After this brief outline of the chronologic cycles, the reader has become familiar with the themes of the mosaics of the Chora Monastery.

Parecclesion or the cemetery chapel is covered with frescoes. The blessed Mary in the dome, Anastasis and the Last Judgment frescoes in the apse semi-dome are unique examples which arouse a deep sense of admiration. Apart from the frescoes, there are four graves in the parecclesion, including that of Theodore Metochites who died in 1332. Including three in the outer narthex and one in the north wall of the inner narthex, there are a total of eight graves in the Chora Monastery.

Theodore Metochites

In the beginning of the 13th century, Europe was preparing for the fourth crusade aiming to go to the holy lands and occupy Jerusalem. However, the fourth crusade had a very different outcome from the one the Pope had preached. The aim of most of the crusaders was to get the treasures of the Byzantium. Due to the provocations of the Venetians who were to play a major part in the coming tragedy, the crusaders never made it to Jerusalem. The army reached the Bosphorus and camped across the straits of Istanbul.

The Emperor Alexios III failing to save the city gathered up his family and his gold pieces, and fled. Finally, the crusaders managed to enter the city on April 13, 1204 and

Detail from the scene of 'Methochite's presentation of the model of the church to Jesus'

Support wall in the east of Kariye Museum and the architecture from outside

started to loot its treasures. There were three days of sack and massacre in the occupied area and this dazzling city was turned into the ruins. They established a new Latin kingdom and installed a Latin ruler, Count Baldwin IX of Flanders, on the throne of Byzantium.

The nobles who fled the city like the emperor established two kingdoms in Anatolia: one in Trabzon and the other in Nicaea. The Kingdom of Nicaea founded by Theodore Laskaris, the son-in-law of Alexius III, accomplished to take Istanbul back from the Latins 57 years later, in 1261. When they returned, they found the city badly damaged.

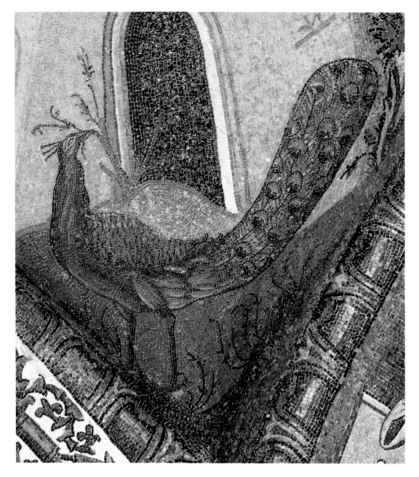

Even the magnificent structures such as Hagia Sophia and Chora Monastery were in ruins. A city which had housed one million people was almost deserted.

Theodore Metochites who would decorate the Chora Monastery with beautiful mosaics and frescoes years later, was born in Niceae in around 1260, one year before Istanbul's taking back from the Latins. His family returned to Istanbul after this event. His father George Metochites was a prominent Eastern Orthodox cleric under the Emperor Michael VIII and a leading advocate of the union with the Latin Church. After the emperor's death, as he insisted on his thoughts, he was excommunicated by the church and banished to Nicea.

Having a good education, Theodore Metochites in his younger days, preferred to stay away from the politics because of the thoughts of his father and dedicated himself to scientific researches. He started to write his collection of tracts and essays on classical thought, history and literature while he was very young, and attracted public attention. As a result, he was presented to the Emperor Andronicus II during one of his trips to Anatolia. Metochites had a chance to present one of his collections, Elegy for Nicaea, to the emperor and impressed him in such a way that, even though his father had fallen in disfavor and was sent to exile, the emperor recruited him in the Palace.

Metochites started to rise quickly in the Byzantine Palace and in a year he acquired the 'Leader of the Communities' title which allowed him to become a member of the senators' class. In 1290, he led an embassy to Cyprus, Cilicia and Serbia arranging marriages of the palace family. In 1303, when the Queen Irene went to Thessalonica to establish a semi-independent administration, Metochites joined her as a prime minister and two years later returned to the capital responsible for the treasury and the state.

Metochites who was elevated to the highest rank in Byzantine, was directing political affairs as well as taking decisions to reward or punish people. At the same time, he acquired a substantial fortune. To secure his position, he arranged the most advantageous marriages for the emperor's sons whom he considered as his political rivals, and continued to keep good relations with them.

In the meantime, he was carrying on his literary works. His protégé Nicephorus Gregoros was describing him as "From the morning till night he directs politics with all efforts as if he has nothing to do with science, but late at night when he leaves the palace starts to dedicate himself to his scientific studies." However, he was being harshly criticized for his scientific and literary works, as well. Nicephorus Khoumnos who was his political rival, was identifying him as an unintelligible author who was repeating himself. In addition, he was blaming him for being a bad astronomer of no use.

Despite all these criticisms and accusations, Metochites with the support of the emperor, continued his studies, with more emphasis on literature. His voluminous writings range from scientific to theological matters. He wrote commentaries on Aristotle, essays, an introduction to astronomy, public addressees and poems for saints. When he was 43 years old, the emperor personally encouraged him to study astronomy.

Mosaics from section I of the inner narthex. At the left end 'Genealogy of Jesus', in the arch next to it 'feeding of Mary', in the vault above 'presentation of Mary to the temple', 'Metochites' presentation of the church to Jesus' below, next to this 'first seven steps of Mary' and on the left end 'Mary being caressed'.

The emperor also asked him to take care of the Chora Monastery. This was a true blessing for him, since he was deeply interested in this monastery _ already living in the neighborhood _ towards the year 1316.

Since the Grand Palace was destroyed during the Latin occupation, the emperors were living in the Blakhernae Palace nearby the Chora Monastery. Formerly, the monastery was under the patronage of the emperor and his family. Metochites demanded from Andronicus II to give the monastery under his protection for restoration, and his request was approved by the emperor. Henceforth, Metochites was acting as if he was an emperor in his social

Isaac Comnenos, son of Byzantine Emperor Alexius I, had repaired the church, therefore he is pictured next to Mary in 'Jesus of the Chalke' mosaic (J65).

life. In 1320, his perpetual rise was continuing. Meantime, he was promoted to 'Megas Logothetes' ('Grand Logothete' or 'Chancellor'). By this means, he organized the hierarchical order in the palace. He was the second most important person in the empire after the emperor with respect to power and wealth. During this gleaming period, he restored and repaired the Chora Monastery and adorned it with the magnificent mosaics between the years 1302 and 1320.

He had a cemetery chapel erected next to the church demonstrating his wealth, power as well as his good taste in art. He also put a mosaic panel of himself in the church

The scene of 'annunciation to St. Anne' that she would have a child; in the panel designated as No. 87 in section G in the north end of the second narthex.

as he offers Jesus a model of the church. In this panel, his long hat and his eye-catching robe ornamented with gold reflect his wealth. In the inscription here, it is written "Ho Ktetor Logothetes tou Genikou Theodoros ho Metochites" (Founder, Chancellor Theodore Metochites).

The Emperor Andronicus II who was ruling for 40 years was getting old. In addition, there were a number of problems and the country was under an uneasy state. The land was being lost to Turks in Anatolia, while the Catalan legions were destroying the country in the west. Big land losses in the Balkans as well as in Anatolia caused the empire to confine to a narrow land surrounded by enemies. The end was close. This also meant the beginning of the tragic end of Metochites who had been in the service of the palace for 30 years. Although he was identified as 'a personified philosophy' by his admirers, his enemies were considering him as an ambitious, arrogant and boring person. But he preferred to stay out of these discussions and the ones pertaining to religion, and had the decoration of the monastery finished.

As years passed by, Metochites' fortune, power and his influence on the emperor were disturbing many. Each day, the number of his enemies including even his own sons was increasing. He was known as 'the Emperor's malicious demon' among the common people. In 1328, there was an unsuccessful attempt to depose him. Although, he managed to survive and save his fortune, he was quite frightened by this event. Not only the people did not like him, but also

they wanted his supporter æ the emperor æ to be deposed by his nephew, young Andronicus. It was the time to step down for Metochites. Finally, young Andronicus captured the city and overthrew the emperor and ascended to the throne as Andronicus III (1328-1341). People wanted Metochites to be blinded with a red-hot iron. However, the new emperor did not perform the public wish. He confiscated his fortune and exiled him to Didymoteikhon in Thrace.

Facing the same faith with his father, Metochites suffered from his poor life there after all those glamorous years. Being hopeless and annoyed, he was ailing. He often wrote letters of excuse to the emperor, and asked for permission to return to the capital. After two years of exile, finally in 1330, he was pardoned and permitted to return to Istanbul where he would spend the rest of his days in melancholy.

The condition of his return was to be a destitute monk in the Chora Monastery for the rest of his life. Even this was a blessing for him and, he accepted the offer at once. He was not called Metochites anymore. He carried on his life as 'Theoleptos the Monk', by writing and praying. Consequently, he died on March 13, 1332 in the Chora Monastery and was buried there, in his tomb in Pareeclesion.

Igor Schevchenco who is a famous researcher on the Byzantine history says for Metochites, "To provide us Chora, he was supposed to be a rich, tasteful, and an intelligent man. It was not necessary for him to be a perfect gentleman". In fact, if we put aside his arrogance and political manipulative behavior which were the prerequisite of the era, he became immortal with the Chora Monastery which he created and adorned with magnificent mosaics. It will not be fair if we do not appreciate Metochites as well as these worldwide famous mosaics.

Palestine when the New Testament was written

Palestine and Middle East when the Old Testament was written

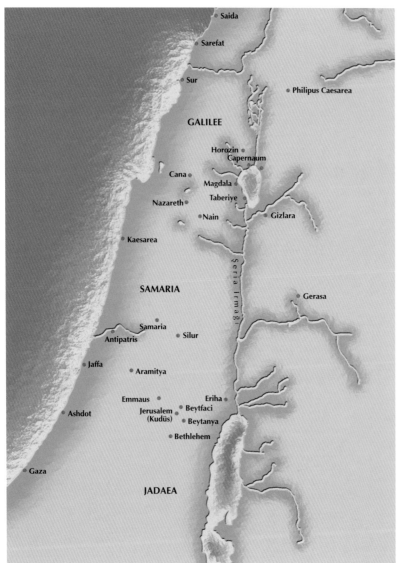

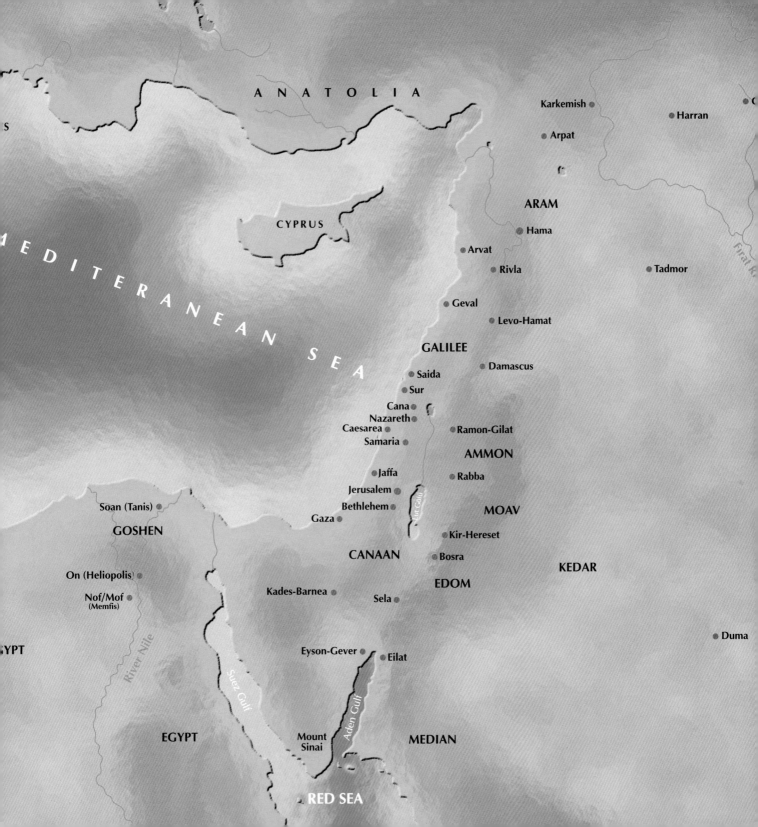

The Journey to Bethlehem

Let us start our tour from the left side of the Chora Museum by tracing the mosaics on the wall at the left end of the outer narthex. In the section denoted as A in our plan, the mosaic No.1 in which three scenes are merged within a single landscape setting has the subject of Virgin Mary's visit to Bethlehem and Joseph's dream. At the left is the scene of Joseph's dreaming. He lies asleep under a small tree. Above, hovering in flight, the angel is breaking him the good news of the birth of Jesus. To the right of this scene, two women appear to be engaged in conversation, one being Mary and the other Elizabeth, the wife of Zachariah. At the right, is the major scene of the composition: the journey to Bethlehem. Leading the way at the far right is one of Joseph's sons and Joseph is following behind the donkey on which Mary is seated. The family is journeying to Bethlehem to be enrolled for the census count. On the background is the landscape of the town.

ΑΝΕΒΗ ΔΕ ΚΑΙ ΙΩ(ΣΗ)Φ ΑΠΟ ΤΗΣ ΓΑΛΙΛΑΙΑΣ ΕΚ ΠΟΛΕΩΣ
ΝΑΖΑΡΕΤ ΕΙΣ ΤΗΝ ΙΟΥΔΑΙΑΝ ΕΙΣ ΠΟΛΙΝ Δ(ΑΥΙ)Δ ΗΤΙΣ ΚΑΛΕΙΤΑΙ
ΒΗΘΛΕΕΜ

ΤΟΥ ΑΠΟΓΡΑΨΑΣΘΑΙ ΣΥΝ ΜΑΡΙΑΜ
ΤΗ ΜΕΜΝΗΣΤΕΥΜΕΝΗ ΑΥΤΩ ΟΥΣΗ ΕΓΚΥΩ

Holy Family's Journey to Jerusalem

The Mosaic No. 2 on the west side of the section A illustrates Jesus Christ going to Jerusalem from Bethlehem for the celebration of Passover with Mary and Joseph. It was always a festive occasion to meet in Jerusalem for Passover and when Jesus was 12 years old, Mary and Joseph took him to Jerusalem. Once the Passover was over they began to journey home and later on noticed that Jesus was missing and became alarmed. When a thorough search of the camp did not reveal Jesus' whereabouts, Joseph and Mary returned to Jerusalem. After three days of visiting relatives and friends in the city, they finally found him in the temple, in the middle of the priests both hearing them and asking questions. Both Mary and Joseph and all the others that heard him were astonished at his understanding and answers. (Luke 2:41-47)

On this panel, certain saints such as Anempodistus, Epideforous, Alphonius, Achidinus and Pegasius are depicted in the medallions. This panel is rather weak in the artistic sense in comparison to the others in the monastery. For example, the grace, well-balance and richness in the preceding panel lack in this one. As the mosaics in the Chora Monastery had been made by different artists, some are exquisite whereas the others are relatively poor.

On the left, one can see buildings with large doors and windows. Jesus, Mary and Joseph are depicted here while entering into Jerusalem.

Enrollment for the Census Count Before Cyrenius

(A-6)

A census count is depicted in the mosaic No. 6, on the east side of the section A. The emperor Augustos has decreed a census count be made in all of the Roman provinces. And since everyone was required to return to the city of his birth, Joseph who was of the house and lineage of David took his fiancé Mary from Nazareth to Bethlehem in Judaea for this enrollment. Cyrenius was the governor of Syria at this time.

The governor Cyrenius is seated on a golden throne. He wears a military cape attached at the right shoulder by a fibula and on his head is a white hat which curves forward to a sharp point. A fully armed military guard stands beside Cyrenius. Standing a little apart and at the center of the scene are a scribe and a second military guard holding a sword and taking part in the interrogation. Mary stands in front of a house with trees nearby and is being enrolled. At the far right stands the nimbed figure of Joseph, with his sons behind him. The inscription of three lines seen in the middle of the panel is the explanation of the subject of the scenes. Being unique in the Eastern Art, this panel is one of the best examples of mosaics in the Chora Museum.

St. Andronicus and St. Tarachus

The mosaics of Tarachus and Andronicus are located in the vault between A and B sections. These two individuals were made saints as they were tortured on the same day, during the period of the Roman Emperor Diocletian (284-305 A.D.). Tarachus was an old but healthy soldier from Cilicia (No.9) and Andronicus was a young man from Ephesus. In the mosaics, Andronicus - denoted - No.1- is shown as a nimbed figure of a young man with a lock of hair hanging down over his forehead and holding a cross in his hand. He wears a red dress and a dark blue himation over it. Opposite to this, Tarachus is shown to be older with a beard and a cross in his hand.

St. Andronicus on the left and St. Tarachus on the right

Return of the Holy Family From Egypt to Nazareth

The mosaic in the inner surface of the outer wall of the church depicts the Holy Family returning from Egypt. Joseph was advised in a dream by an angel that they should flee into Egypt and stay there until the danger passed. Joseph then woke up and took Mary and Jesus to Egypt, at once. The panel depicting the journey to Egypt was in K section. However it could not survive to the present day. The Holy Family lived in Egypt for 4 years. In another dream of Joseph, when he was in Egypt an angel commanded him to take Mary and the Christ child back to Israel, since those who had sought to take the child's life were dead (Matthew 2:12-22). Following to this, the family departed. On this panel, the town of Nazareth is seen at the right. At the left Joseph is stretched out on a pallet and is sleeping. In the middle, one can see the donkey prepared for the trip and Mary and Joseph carrying the child on his shoulders. Although the family was on the way to Jerusalem, Joseph feared to proceed because he had learned that Archelaus, son of Herod, as cruel as his father, had succeeded his father in Judaea. In the later dream, Joseph was warned to turn "aside into the parts of Galilee" and went to the Galilean city of Nazareth, where they were to dwell. The subject has been depicted on this mosaic skillfully in a very harmonious manner. The depictions of Philemon, Lucius, Collnicus, Tirsus, and Apollinus are found above the arched vault.

The panel showing the Holy Family's return from Egypt to Nazareth
The scene of Joseph carrying Jesus on his shoulders, from the same panel

Jesus' Baptism and the Temptation of Christ

The subject of Satan tempting Jesus has been taken up on the ceiling in the B section of the Chora Museum. Subjects are developed around a medallion in the center. One can see Jesus being baptized in the Jordan river by John the Baptist in one corner of the dome. Before describing the scene of the baptism of Jesus, let us here give some information on John the Baptist.

In the days of King Herod, there was a priest named Zachariah in Judaea. He and his wife Elizabeth were very old and had no child. For this reason, they were both grieving. One day an angel appeared to Zachariah with the astounding news that Elizabeth, though long past the age for child bearing, would give him a son to be called John. Elizabeth had conceived as the angel had predicted and then gave birth to a son. They named him as John. John grew up. It was the 15th year of the reign of the Roman Emperor Tiberius and Herod Antipas was the King of Galilee and Pontius Pilate the governor of Judaea. God had spoken to John in the desert. Then John walked all around the Jordan river preaching the baptism of repentance for the remissions of the sins. All the people of Judaea and Jerusalem followed him, confessed their sins and were baptized with the waters of the Jordan river. And, as the people were in expectation, they asked him if he was a 'Messiah' or not. John answered them saying "I indeed baptize you with water; but one mightier than I will come and will baptize you with the Holy

The scene of John the Baptist baptizing Jesus in the Jordan River

Ghost and with fire."

While John was baptizing the people in the Jordan River, Jesus came to John to be baptized. It was a dramatic moment as the two men faced each other. John recognized him immediately. "I have need to be baptized by you." He resisted humbly. "Suffer it as it is now" Jesus answered, "For thus it becomes us to fulfill all righteousness." Following to this, John baptized Jesus. As Jesus stood in the water after his baptism he saw a vision like the spirit of God in the shape of a white dove descending to light upon his shoulder (Matthew 3:13-16)

Let us mention the death of him and conclude the life story of John. Herod Antipas, had married the wife of his brother. For this, John forthrightly denounced him. For this reason, Herod was nursing a grudge against him. He imprisoned John and was looking for a pretext to have him killed. When he was giving a great feast to which the rich and noble in the tetrarchy were invited, in his birthday, his step daughter Salome danced for him and the guests. The king and the guests were impressed by her dance. After the dance, Herod drunkenly promised to give the girl whatever she asked. Instructed by her mother, Salome asked for the head of John the Baptist. Herod was troubled and afraid, but being a vain man, he was also reluctant to be shamed for not carrying out his oath. He ordered to behead John and bring his head to the girl. This was the tragic end of John the Baptist (Mark 6:21-28)

In the scenes, John the Baptist is depicted wearing sheep's pelt symbolizing the long-suffering life spent in the desert. In the panel in the dome, again he can be seen with sheep's pelt while the Jordan River is below. The multitude behind John seems like talking to him. There is a tree between him and Jesus.

Jesus' coming to John the Baptist to be baptized

After the baptism of Jesus, the Holy Spirit wished to test him and brought him to the desert. Jesus fasted in the desert for 40 consecutive days and nights and finally felt hungry. At this point, he was tempted by the voice of evil who said "If you are the son of God, command that these stones be made into bread." But Jesus answered without hesitation "It is written, 'Man shall not live by bread alone, but by every word that proceeds out of the mouth of God.'" Then Satan took Jesus to the hills of Jerusalem. As he stood in the highest place of the temple the evil voice spoke again. "If you are the son of God, cast yourself down" the voice said. "For it is written, 'He shall give his angels charge concerning you and in their hands they shall bear you up, lest any time you dash your foot against a stone'". Jesus answered this temptation, too as he had the other "It is written again, 'You shall not tempt the Lord your God'" Then, Satan took him to a mountain top and showed him all the kingdoms of the world and the glory of them and offered him all those things if he would fall down and worship him. Then Jesus said unto him "Go your way Satan; You shall worship the Lord your God, and him only you shall serve." Defeated, the devil left him and angels came and ministered unto him. (Matthew 4:1-11, Mark 1:12-13, Luke 4:11-13)

In the mosaics of the temptation (No 15, 16) in the vault in the B section, the subjects are depicted around a medallion which is located at the center. The inscriptions above the figure describe the events. In the lower left corner of the dome, John the Baptist with a multitude behind him and Jesus who came to be baptized can be seen. John seems as if he is addressing to the multitude whereas in the other parts, Satan is seen trying to tempt Jesus. The devil is portrayed as a dark, winged and ugly creature. On both sides of this scene, the depictions of the saints can be seen.

The scene of 'temptation of Jesus' in the vault in section B in the outer narthex. Below the panel is the baptism of Jesus and above are the scenes of Satan's temptations

The Birth of Christ

The birth of Jesus Christ is the subject of the mosaic shown as No. 17 in the B section. This panel shows the events related to the birth of Christ. At this point, let us go back to the story of Mary's journey to Bethlehem and Joseph's dream, in order for us to remember the events before Jesus' birth.

Joseph and Mary were engaged. However, Mary conceived

The scene of 'annunciation to Mary at the well' that she would have a child from the Holy Spirit, in the north of the inner narthex (G 90)

The scene of 'Christ's birth'

with the Holy Spirit. Joseph found it hard to believe her story of the visit from the angel. While he was thinking of a way to break off the engagement, an angel appeared to him in a dream. "Joseph, son of David," the angel said, "Fear not to take Mary as your wife, for that which is conceived in her is of the Holy Ghost. She shall bring forth a son and you shall call his name Jesus, for he shall save the people from their sins." No longer doubting then, Joseph quitted the idea of breaking off the engagement. After a while, Joseph and Mary went to Bethlehem to enroll for the census count. Meantime, the day has come. Since they couldn't find a place in the inn, the couple was forced to take refuge in a stable. There Mary gave birth to a son. The shepherds abiding in the mountains and the three Magi from the East were the ones who first worshipped Christ.

In the mosaic, the ox and the ass are shown as they peer at the child in the manger. At the far left, a woman stands and pours water from a golden vessel into a large golden basin raised on a pedestal. Another woman sits facing the basin from the opposite side and holds the infant Jesus in her lap to give him a bath. In the center of the composition Mary is lying on a pallet after giving birth, and a ray of light shines directly down upon swaddled Jesus. Behind the Virgin is a group of angels. To the right, are three shepherds behind the sheep, one of whom is standing while the other two are seated. An angel has descended to announce them the birth of Christ. Joseph is depicted sitting in the lower corner and watching the bathing of the infant.

Depictions of St. George and St. Demetrius

B-C 20 / C-D 27

The depictions of St. George (No. 20) and St. Demetrius (No. 27) can be seen in the bays between the sections B-C and C-D of the outer narthex. However, these depictions are partly deteriorated. The father of St. George was from Cappadocia. He was born towards the end of the 3rd century. When it was found out that he was a Christian in the time of the Roman Emperor Diocletianus (284-305 A.D.), he was tortured and executed in the year 296. St. Demetrius was from Thessalonica. When the Roman Emperor Maximianus (235-238 A.D.) came to Thessalonica, he imposed a death sentence upon Demetrius, whom he saw amongst the Christians. For these reasons, these two saints are pictured facing each other in the vault.

An unidentified saint figure since the head is lost, on the left, St George on the right

Next Pages: In the arches of the B section of the outer narthex St George and St Demetrius. Below the arch is the scene of Birth of Jesus and in the vault is the Temptation of Jesus

Christ Pantocrator

There is a monumental image of Jesus Christ above the entrance to the inner narthex, just opposite to the entrance gate of the museum. As soon as one enters into the museum he or she confronts with this striking mosaic. Here, Christ is shown clutching the Book of the Gospels to his bosom with his left hand and making a gesture of blessing with his right. This type of image is that of Christ Pantocrator, which means 'Lord of the Universe'. In this masterpiece, Jesus appears with his hair carefully parted in the middle, and his face presents a spiritual appearance.

Jesus was depicted as a young man without beard in the descriptions until the end of the 5th century. However, after the 6th century in all pictures and mosaics, illustrations, frescoes, icons, throughout all Byzantium art, he was depicted as a middle-aged man with thick hair and beard. The monogram of Jesus on both sides of his head, the inscriptions which read "Chora" in the lower section and "Jesus Christ, the dwelling place of the living" in the left section accompany the image. Philosophically, the phrase was taken from the Bible as a play upon the name of the monastery. In *The Calendar of the Saints of the Orthodox Church* written in the 11th century by Simeon Metaphrates, an incident that had happened in Urfa was described: Jesus after washing his face wipes it with a towel and gives the towel to the painter called Ananias who has been trying to portray him, and the towel has been imprinted by the image of Jesus' face. From that day on, Jesus was depicted as a middle-aged man.

'Christ Pantocrator' mosaic above the door leading to the inner narthex

The Virgin Blachernitissa and Angels

Above the entrance door of the Chora Museum is the figure of the Virgin between two angels. The Virgin is of the type of the Blachernitissa, so called because its prototype is believed to have been an icon in the Blachernae Monastery which is located in the Ayvansaray quarter of Istanbul. Here, the Virgin, at the center, with the infant Jesus which appears in an ovoid shape on her breast, stands in a dignified and calm manner with arms stretched upwards and praying. This symbolizes that her bosom is greater than the universe. Admirably fitted into the sides of the arch are two flying angels each with a halo over the head, as they approach Mary. The mosaicist who was able to animate the scene by rendering a sense of motion to the angels was, most probably, one of the most talented among the mosaicists who decorated the church.

In the inscription in the mosaic one can read "The Mother of God, the dwelling place of the uncontainable". There is the scene of the multiplication of loaves by Christ, above the deteriorated figures of two saints in the bay on both sides of this panel. Again in the other corner of this panel, there is a scene of sacrificing of a bull.

The Virgin Blachenitissa and the angels. Above the panel on the left is the scene of 'multiplication of bread' and on the right is the scene of 'sacrificing of a bull'

Water Being Turned Into Wine and Multiplication of Loaves

The scene of Christ's first miracle, turning of the water into wine is found above the section between the museum's entrance gate and the gate leading to the inner narthex.

Jesus Christ, his mother Mary and the Apostles were invited to a wedding in the town of Cana in Galilee. When it was noticed that they ran out of wine at the wedding, Mary came to her son, saying that they had run out of wine. Jesus instructed the servants to fill the six water pots in the house with water. Then Jesus asked them to carry some of the water to the governor of the feast. After the governor tasted the cup, he sent the servants to pour wine for the guests while he drew the bride-groom aside and said "You kept the best wine until now." After this miraculous event there, people worshipped him. Christ's first miracle, turning of water into wine, is the subject of the mosaic here. One of the servants pours water into one of the water pots in the back row. On the right, the other servant approaches with a clay amphora supported on his shoulder. The governor of the feast presents the tumbler. Mary, Peter and John stand next to Jesus witnessing this first of an extensive series of miracles.

The miracle of 'water being turned to wine': one is filling the water pots while the other is carrying water, the governor of the feast showing the quality of the wine

After the beheading of John, Jesus went to a desert place. The people who have heard his miracles of healing the sick were following him. The time for Passover was approaching, when the Jews celebrate the deliverance from slavery in Egypt to the land of Promise. Jesus embarked in a mountaintop and sat with his disciples. As always, the people followed and Jesus began to heal the sick and cripple, deaf and blind. As the darkness approached Jesus showed no sign of dismissing the crowd. His disciples came to him saying "This is a desert place and the time is now past. Send the multitude away, that they may go to the villages and buy themselves victuals."

But Jesus said without stopping his work "Give them food".

"Shall we buy 200 penny worth of bread and give them that?" Philip asked scornfully.

"Go and see how many loaves you have," Jesus ordered.

"We have here five loaves and two fish," said Peter's brother, Andreas.

He commanded them to divide the people into companies of fifty and while this was being done, he took five loaves and two fish blessing and breaking them in his hands and he gave the loaves to his disciples who in their turn gave them to the multitude. And they did all eat and were filled. The disciples gathered the fragments that remained in 12 baskets. People seeing this happen believed that he was the Messiah they have been waiting for. (Matthew 14:9-20, 15:29-39)

This event is depicted in the mosaic as one can see the baskets which are full of loaves of bread.

Detail showing the spreading of bread in the scene of 'multiplication of loaves'

The Flight of Elizabeth and John From a Soldier

To right of the entrance gate, on the panel of the inner side of the outer wall, Elizabeth and John are seen fleeing from a soldier who is chasing them with a sword in his hand. They survived by finding sanctuary in the mountain. Elizabeth is a relative of Mary, the wife of Zachariah and the mother of John the Baptist. The mosaics in the dome are lost in this section. Saints are depicted between the D and A sections, right next to this and above the bay. Since the mosaics have fallen, it is not possible to identify them. In a deteriorated decoration of a scene on the wall of the inner narthex in the E section 'the interrogation of the King Herod' is depicted. A guard is shown as interrogating a woman.

The panel above the east wall of the museum's outer narthex shows King Herod issuing the command for the slaying of newborn children, since he had been told that a newborn child would overturn his throne. Across from this, is a mosaic of mothers mourning. Unfortunately, the mosaics in the middle and side bays have disappeared. Here, only in the panel designated as E-40, King Herod is shown sitting on his throne with a guard behind him.

Jesus and the Samaritan Woman

A view from the scene of the 'massacre of the innocents' (F43)

The survived section of the scene of 'the interrogation of King Herod'. The rest could not survive to the present day

In the northern corner of the section in the right end is the scene of Jesus conversing with the Samaritan woman figure. However, this mosaic is in a very poor state and one can see only the figure of the woman.

Jesus one day left Judaea and departed to Galilee. He had to go through Samaria. Later, he arrived to the town Sychar in Samaria. Samaritans, living in between Judaea and Galilee, were of a hybrid race formed by Jews mixing with other races. For this reason, they were regarded with disdain by the Jews. Jesus and his disciples were tired. As his disciples had gone to the city to buy food, Jesus was alone, sitting next to a well and resting. It was around noon time, there came a Samaritan woman to draw water. Jesus said to her "give me to drink" and the Samaritan woman said "How is that you, being a Jew asked drink of me, which I am a woman of Samaria?" Jesus answered "If you knew the gift of God and who it is that said to you, 'Give me to drink', you would have asked of him, and he would have given to you the living water." The woman said: "Sir you have nothing to draw water with and the well is deep; from where will you find that living water? Are you greater than our father Jacob who gave us the well and drank thereof himself and his children and his cattle?" This place was near to the parcel of ground that Jacob gave to his son Joseph. The woman was mentioning this. Upon this Jesus answered "Whoever drinks of this water will thirst again, but whoever drinks of the water that I will give him will never thirst, but the water that I will give him will be in him a well of water springing up into everlasting life." the woman said "I know that Messiah will come and he will tell us everything." Jesus said to her "I who speak to you am him."

After this encounter, the woman left her water pot, went her way to the city and called the people and many Samaritans of that city believed Christ. (John 4:3-40)

ΤΟ ΤΕΝ ΕΓΔΗ[.]ΙϹ ΟΤ ΟΝΕϹ ΠΙΧΟΡΥΠ[
ΛΙΝ ΚΑΠΟΤΑΛΙΟ ΔΙΟΑϹΕΝ ΤΟΠΠΑ[
Κ ΕΝ ΠΑΟ ΓΟΘΟΡΟϹ Α ΠϹΑ ΠΟΓΟΚΒ[

King Herod Commanding the Massacre of the Innocents

On the southern wall of the outer narthex of the museum is the scene of King Herod giving the command for the massacre of the innocents. At the time Jesus was born, three wise men (D-34) from the East, informed the king that a child was born in Bethlehem and that child would lead the people of Israel. They were then sent to Bethlehem to find the child. After they had found Mary and infant Jesus, they were warned by God in a dream that they should not go back to Herod. So, they left for their own country by another route.

Joseph was warned in a dream by an angel that they should flee into Egypt where the king could not harm the infant. In the morning, they left Bethlehem at once. Then Herod, discovering that he had been betrayed by the wise men, commanded that all children under the age of two be executed in Bethlehem and its environs. (Matthew 2:16)

Here, in this mosaic, this subject is illustrated. Herod, on his throne turns to the soldiers and gives the command. In the opposite part of the mosaic, soldiers putting his orders into effect and weeping mothers can be seen.

Above this scene is Jesus Christ healing the paralytic in Capernaum and just across this, is the paralytic being healed and carrying his pallet. Opposite to these mosaics, a Samaritan woman is shown at the edge of a well.

The scene of King Herod Commanding the Massacre of the Innocent

In the dome of the F section is the scene of Christ Healing a paralytic and the complete panel of the massacre of the Innocent is below

Christ Healing the Paralytic

F-47

The scene of Christ healing the paralytic at Capernaum is shown in the dome of the section in the right end of the outer narthex.

Jesus had returned to Capernaum for the Sabbath and when his presence became known, the area around Peter's house where he was staying was quickly filled with people. He was telling them the word of God. A paralyzed man was unable to reach the house and hired four men to pick up the pallet upon which he lay and carry him to Jesus. They came to Peter's house and removing the tiles over the porch let the suffering man down through the opening. Jesus saw the faith which had led the petitioner to take such an unconventional way to reach him and said "Son, your sins are forgiven."

"Blasphemy!" thought some priests who were listening, "The Nazarene claims to forgive sins, and this only the God can do." Jesus understood what they had been thinking and turned to the paralyzed man "Arise," he said, "I say to you take up your bed and go to your house." When the sick man rolled up his pallet and put it upon his shoulders, the crowd marveled and glorified God, saying "We have seen strange things today." (Matthew 9:1-8, Luke 5:17-26)

The mosaic depicting this story was covering a large section, but unfortunately, the mosaics in the both sides are totally missing.

The Massacre of the Innocents

The panel of the massacre of the innocents is next to the scene of the healing of a paralytic on the ceiling of the outer narthex of the museum. Herod has commanded for the execution of the innocents and the soldiers obeying to the order are slaying the children. At the left of the panel, a soldier stoops over a child lying flat on its back and is about to thrust his sword into its neck. Next to this, is another soldier in the pursuit of a mother who is holding a small child. In the upper zone one can see another soldier who has transfixed a child on the point of his sword, while the mother of the infant, who is screaming runs towards the soldier in order to save her child. Unfortunately, the center of the panel has been lost. Other soldiers are shown as they are slaying the children in the rest of the panel. Another woman is being threatened by a soldier and just next to this is the Samaritan woman at the edge of a well (F-42).

On the side walls under the dome in which is the scene of healing of a paralytic, one can see Herod giving the order of the massacre of the innocents and soldiers obeying the order. To the southeast of this section is the scene of Christ healing a paralytic in Bethsaida pool where the paralytic is depicted as he is putting his pallet upon his shoulders and departing (F-46).

Soldiers are fulfilling the order of the massacre of the innocents. On the left is a slaying of a child with a sword

A child taken from his mother is being stabbed by a soldier before the mother

The Three Magi From the East Before King Herod

In the section to the right of the entrance gate, the three Magi are shown in the presence of King Herod on the inner narthex wall.

At the time Jesus was born, three wise men (astrologists) from the East, one day appeared in Jerusalem. They asked the question which had brought them there: "Where is he that is born King of the Jews? In pursuit of his star in the East, we have come to worship him."

The question of the Magi started a fear in Herod's heart who had been designated as the king of the Jews by Rome and ruled Palestine between 40 B.C. and 4 A.D. Herod called together the chief priests and the oracles. When he asked them where the Messiah would be born, the answer was the town of Bethlehem in Judaea. The King then ordered the three Magi to go to find that child and to bring him the word where the child might be found so that he could worship him, and he sent them to Bethlehem.

The star guided the Magi to the place Jesus was born. When they found Mary and infant Jesus, they prostrated and worshipped them. Being warned by God in a dream, they did not go back to Herod and returned their own country by another route.

In the mosaic, King Herod seated on a throne turns toward the Magi in a gesture of speaking. An armed guard stands behind him. The first Magus on the right was depicted as an old man with a long, gray beard, the one in the middle is represented as a middle-aged man with a short, dark beard, while the third one is a beardless youth. And the star is seen within a circle in the sky. Behind the three Magi there is a scene in which the three Magi mounted on horses ride over a trail in pursuit of the star. Above this composition are the medallions of three saints.

Three Magi named Melkior, Gaspar, Baltazar had learned the birth of Jesus. They wanted to learn his birthplace before King Herod. Later they found Jesus and worshipped him and returned to their country by a different route.

The foundation of southern section of the Kariye Museum

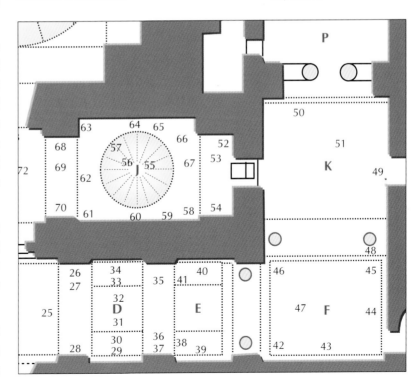

Christ Healing a Leper and the Man with the Withered Hand

The mosaic in the western side of the southern arch of the inner narthex illustrates Christ healing a leper. When he came down from the mountain, a great multitude followed him. And there came a leper and worshipped him saying "Lord, if you will you can make me clean." Then Jesus put forward his hand and touched him saying "I will, be clean". And immediately, his leprosy was cleaned. Then Jesus said to him "Tell no man; but go your way, show yourself to the priest, and offer the gift that Moses commanded, for a testimony unto them." (Matthew 8:1-4)

The leper is depicted wearing only a loincloth and with spots on his body to demonstrate his sickness. The upper parts of Christ and the disciples are now destroyed and only their legs can be seen.

The scene of Christ healing the man with the withered hand is at the opposite side of the scene of Christ healing a leper. (J-53) Jesus entered into the synagogue and saw a man whose right hand was withered. He said to the man "Rise up and stand forth in the midst." Then Jesus said to the crowd "I will ask you one thing: Is it lawful on the Sabbath days to do good or to do evil? To save life or to destroy it?" When no response came from the crowd he was saddened and he asked the man to stretch forth his hand and his hand was restored. (Luke 6:6-10)

Scenes of the miracles of 'healing a leper and a man with the withered hand'

The Genealogy of Christ

J/55-56-57

The inner surfaces of the dome in this section are decorated with mosaics representing the ancestors of Christ, surrounding the medallion of Christ, depicted in the type of the Pantocrator i.e. holding the Bible in his left hand and making a sign of consecration with his right hand. The twenty four forefathers from the prophet Adam to Jacob are shown here separately down to the level of the windows which are placed in the drums of the dome, whereas Jacob's fifteen children are depicted below as a second generation.

Placed skillfully in the flutes, the names of the twenty four ancestors of Christ are as follows: Adam, Seth, Noah, Cainan, Maleleel, Jared, Lamech, Sem, Japheth, Arphaxad, Sala, Heber, Saruch, Nachor, Thar, Abraham, Isaac, Jacob, Phalec, Ragau, Mathusala, Enoch, Enos and Abel. These names are inscripted above the figures.

In the pendentives of this dome, one can see the first four miracles of Jesus. These are Christ healing two blind men, a paralytic and a blind and dumb man. Next to these is another panel of Christ healing a multitude, whereas in the arch is a scene of Christ healing a man with withered hand and a leper.

On the 4 corners of the pendentives of the dome are the other miracles of Jesus

'Genealogy of Christ' in the dome in the south of the inner narthex

Christ Healing a Blind and Dumb Man

In the southwest pendentive of the dome of the Ancestors is the scene of Christ healing a blind and dumb man. They brought to him a person who was possessed by a devil, blind and dumb. And he healed him. The man both spoke and saw. And all the people were amazed and said "Is not this the son of David?" But when the Pharisees heard it, they said this fellow casted out devils by the force of the prince of the devils, Beel Zebub.

And Jesus knew their thoughts and said to them "Every kingdom divided against itself is brought to desolation, and every city or house divided against itself shall not stand. And if Satan cast out Satan he is divided against itself. How shall then his kingdom stand?" (Matthew 12:22-26)

In the mosaic, the afflicted wears a knee-length tunic and his hand is pointing toward his blind eyes. Christ stands at the right with Peter on his left and a young disciple behind.

Christ Healing the Multitude

On the western wall of this section, the scene of Jesus healing the multitude can be found. Jesus went up a mountain and sat down there. And great multitudes came unto him, having with them those who were lame, blind, maimed and many others, and he healed them. (Matthew 15:29-30)

In the mosaic, three men are seated on the ground. The first of the afflicted is a blind cripple holding a hand crutch. The second is a blind man and a third has a greatly distended tumor. In the background behind the group of the seated men, there stands a woman leaning forward and holding her child - whose legs seem to be deformed - out toward Jesus.

Still further in the background is a second woman with her child. At the far right is a figure of a crippled man and are two women æthe one in the front leans on a short stick and the second is blind. Christ followed by disciples is blessing and healing them. The scene is laid in a hilly landscape; a tree and houses are seen in the background.

One of the miracles of Jesus is 'healing of a blind and dumb man'

Detail from the scene of 'the healing of the multitude'

Back page: 'healing of the multitude' scene

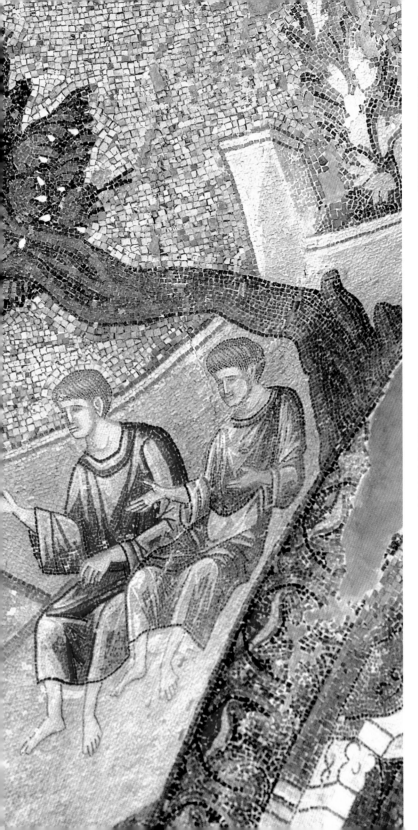

Christ Healing Two Blind Men

I n the southwestern pendentive of this section is the scene of Christ healing two blind men. As they departed from Jericho, a great multitude followed him. And two blind men sitting by the way side cried out saying "Have mercy on us, O Lord You son of David" and followed him. Then Jesus said to them "What is your will that I shall do unto you?" They said "Lord, our eyes may be opened." So Jesus touched their eyes and immediately, their eyes received sight. (Matthew 20:29-34)

Christ Healing the Mother-in-Law of Peter

I n the northeastern pendentive is the scene of Christ healing Peter's mother-in-law. When Jesus entered into the house of Peter, he saw his wife's mother lying sick of fever. He touched her hand and the fever was gone. Then she arose and ministered him. In the mosaic Peter's mother-in-law lies on her bed. Peter stands close beside her. Christ leans forward extending his right arm to grasp the hand of the woman. Two disciples can be seen behind Jesus. The artist had added a door in order to demonstrate the interior of the house.

'Healing of two blind men'
On the next page is 'the healing of the mother-in-law of Peter' scene

The Mosaic of Christ of the Chalke and Virgin Mary

On the eastern wall of the section in which is the dome of the Ancestors are the mosaics of Jesus Christ and Virgin Mary. Although, some of the mosaics are lost in the lower section, one can see an exquisite mosaic of Jesus here. The Prince Isaac Comnenos is represented kneeled down below the praying Virgin whereas Melane, the nun and daughter of Michael Palailogos VIII is on the right side of Jesus.

Isaac Comnenos who was the youngest son of Alexius Comnenos, was the one who had the eastern side of the church repaired. For this reason, he must have been depicted near the Virgin. In addition, he had a tomb prepared for himself in the church, but later he erected a monastery in Thrace near the coast of the river Meric and was buried in there. His tomb was taken there. The Princess Melane who was pictured next to Jesus, was married to the Mongolian Prince Abaga Khan, and later returned to Istanbul upon the death of her husband and became a nun. The inscription indicates that she was "the Lady of Mongols".

Christ is portrayed in the manner of the famous icon that stood above the Chalke Gate, the principal gateway to the Great Palace of Byzantium, and therefore named as Christos Chalkites.

Healing Woman With the Issue of Blood

The miracles of Christ are depicted in the four pendentives of the dome of the Ancestors. The scene of healing of a woman with the issue of blood is found in the southeastern pendentive.

There came a man named Jairus; he was a ruler of the synagogue, and he fell down at Jesus' feet and besought him that he would come to his house. For he had only one daughter about twelve years old and she was dying. As Jesus went, people followed him.

And a woman having an issue of blood for 12 years, who

A woman, thinking that she can be cured if she touches Jesus, is touching Jesus and is cured

had spent all her living upon the physicians, neither could be healed of any, came behind him and touched the border of Jesus' garment; and immediately, her issue of blood stanched. And Jesus said "Who touched me?" When all denied, Peter said "Master, the multitude throng you and pressed you." And Jesus said "Somebody touched me for I perceive that virtue is gone out of me." And when the woman saw that she was not hid, she declared for what cause she had touched him. And Jesus said, "Daughter, be of good comfort; your faith had saved you, go in peace." Then there came one from the ruler of the synagogue's house saying "Your daughter is dead, trouble not the Master." But when Jesus heard it, he answered him saying "Fear not; believe only and she will be cured." And when he came to the house, he suffered no man to go in but Peter, James, John and the parents of the maiden. And they laughed him. He put them all out and took her by the hand and called "Maid, arise". Then she arose and he commanded to give her food. (Luke 8:41-55)

In the scene, the woman with the issue of blood is pressing through the crowd behind him and touching the hem of his garment while Jesus is on the way to the house of Jairus. Jesus turns the upper part of his body, looking back at the woman dressed in black. On the far right one sees three men wearing red and dark blue dresses.

Ο ΧC ΙΩΜ[ΕΝΟC] [Τ]ΗΝ ΑΙΜΟΡΡΟ[Υ]Ν

ΙC ΧC

Mosaics of St. Peter and St. Paul

J-I 68 / H-I 74

Mosaics of St. Peter and St. Paul are found in the inner narthex on either side of the gate to the naos. To the right of the gate St. Paul is depicted in an arched frame. He is shown holding a book in his left hand and his right hand is raised in the air making a gesture of teaching with the tip of the ring finger touching the tip of the thumb. He wears a blue tunic. The mosaicist had skillfully rendered to give the expression of his face.

St. Paul from Tarsus was originally a Jew. His father and mother were of the Jews of the Roman citizens. His real name was Saul. He had been sent to Damascus to destroy a small Christian community, but suddenly he was blinded by a ray of light from the sky and fell down and heard a voice say "Saul, You are betraying me" St. Paul then asked "Who are you?" The voice said "I am Jesus." After he received his sight back, he was baptized and he changed his name and joined to Jesus' closest apostles. He was put in custody in Palestine during the period of the Roman Emperor Nero (54-68 A.D) and subsequently, sent to Rome where he was killed.

On the left is Apostle Peter and on the right is Paul

To the left of the gate is the mosaic of St. Peter who once earned his livelihood as a fisherman. Jesus approached him one day while he was repairing his net. Inspired by his thoughts he became a loyal Apostle. Jesus said to him "You will build my church on this Earth and I will give you the keys of the kingdom of Heaven." (Matthew 16:19). And he built the first Christian churches with St. Paul. He spread Christianity in Anatolia, especially in Antioch. Then he established the first Christian community in Rome. After working 25 years, he was blamed for sorcery. While he was fleeing the city upon the advise of the ones who were close to him, he saw a vision of Jesus and asked him "Domine, Quo Vadis (Where are you going to?)" and Jesus answered "I am going to Rome to be crucified again" Following to this, he returned to Rome where he was arrested and crucified. He is depicted in the mosaic holding a scroll of a letter he wrote in his right hand and in his left hand he seems to be holding the keys to Heaven.

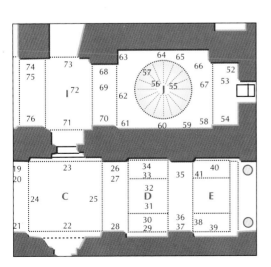

The Virgin Fed by an Angel and Presentation of the Virgin in the Temple

JI-69 / I-72

On the arch to the right of the principle entrance to the nave, the incident of Mary being fed by an angel is illustrated. Mary is seated on the throne with four poles in the holy place of the temple. An angel in flight offers her bread. Only the High Priest could enter here once a year. Mary looking at the angel stretches forth her hand to take the bread.

Mary's parents had promised to leave her in a temple if they had a child. Therefore, Mary was left in the care of the temple. She stayed in the temple for 12 years, and was being daily nourished the heavenly bread by an angel. When she reached the age of 15, she was engaged with Joseph whose rod began to sprout green leaves. Above this scene is the parade of the virgins. These joyful, young maidens with different attires, postures and holding torches in their hands are pictured in motion.

Previous page: Virgins' parade in the scene of 'the presentation to the temple'

Left: The scene of 'Mary being fed by an angel'

Right: The scene of 'Mary's presentation to the temple'

The Virgin Receiving Skein of Wool From Temple

I-71

Above the gate that leads from the outer narthex to the inner narthex is the scene of Mary taking some wool to knit the veils for the temple.

As we have mentioned in the previous section, Mary's parents had promised to leave her in a temple if they had a child. Therefore, Mary was presented to the temple and stayed there for 12 years, until she reached the age of 15. During this period, she was trained while she was ministering to the temple. As it is seen in the mosaic, she knits the veils of the temple.

On the left, three priests are seated on a curved bench. The priest on the right, nearest to the center of the panel, is depicted as if he is about to present the skein of pink wool to Mary who stands in the center of the composition, with a halo over her head, clad in a long blue dress. Six virgins stand behind her; they are depicted in colored dresses while they are watching the scene.

Both the naturalness in the people's appearance and actions as well as the harmony in the colors of this panel indicate that the artist who painted it was extremely skilled at what he was doing.

Detail from the scene of 'Mary receiving a skein of wool from the temple'

The Virgin
Blessed by Priests

On the ceiling of the second bay of the inner narthex are two scenes located at the sides of a medallion which is in the middle. On one side Mary is depicted between her parents. Mary is caressed by Anna and Joachim who are seated symmetrically near a house with a peacock in front of its door. A young woman emerges from the house on the right, stretching forward her arms as if she would take Mary, while on the other side another young woman stands next to a peacock and watches the scene.

On the opposite side of the medallion Joachim brings Mary to the priests to be blessed. Joachim on the left, wearing a light blue tunic, advances to receive the benediction from three high priests who are seated around a table and waiting for him.

The mosaics here which are not damaged are multi-colored and the most striking ones in the Chora Museum.

On the arch between the adjoining bay and this one, are the scenes of the first seven steps of Mary and Head Priest Zachariah praying before the twelve rods of the suitors.

Mary is being caressed by her parents
The scene of 'Mary being taken to the temple for the blessing'

Metochites Presenting the Model of the Church to Christ

Above the gate which opens out into the nave is a panel that shows Theodor Metochites as he gives Jesus a model of the church. Jesus, wearing a large tunic is seated on a throne. Resting on his left thigh is the closed Book of the Gospels which he holds with his left hand. He raises his right hand before him in blessing.

On the left, kneeling and offering his church to Christ, is Theodor Metochites. Metochites wearing a patterned caftan with a high and widely spreading turban covered with a fabric is portrayed with a long square-cut beard.

Although the model of the church is presented to Christ, the artist was not able to guide the look of Christ in the correct direction. Perhaps he did it on purpose because of his deep respect to him. A slight turn of the head would fix this where the rest of the scene is perfectly depicted.

As mentioned in the previous chapters, Metochites as a statesman, a scholar and a poet, was an outstanding man of his time. He had the church repaired between 1302 and 1320 and ornamented with precious mosaics and frescoes. At the same time, he served as the controller of the general treasury of the Emperor Andronicus II. This title of his is inscripted on the mosaic near his head.

The scene of Metochites' Presentation of the Model of the Church to Jesus

The Presentation scene and above is the panel of Presentation of Mary to the Temple

Mary's Engagement with Joseph

On the southern wall of the second section in the inner narthex are the mosaics illustrating Joseph's rod sprouting green leaves which indicates that Joseph is designated as Mary's husband by the God. In this scene Zachariah stands in front of a domed altar over four columns, holding Joseph's flowered rod in his right hand. The suitor whose rod produces a flower will take Mary as a wife. Hence, Joseph is the one. Next to Zachariah stands Mary with a halo whereas Joseph and the other suitors are on the opposite side.

As it is known, Joachim had promised to leave his child in a temple if he had one. He kept his promise and left Mary in the care of the temple. After Mary's ministering to God in the temple for 12 years, the priests announced that it was the time for her to get married, when she reached the age of 15. Head Priest Zachariah called the suitors together and placed their rods on the altar, praying for a sign indicating to whom she should be given. They all gathered at the temple one night. When morning came, the rod of Joseph, a carpenter from Nazareth, began to sprout green leaves and Mary was entrusted to him. This subject is depicted in the mosaics here.

The scene of Mary's Engagement with Joseph. At the left is the detail from the same scene, showing the Head Priest Zachariah and Mary. Zachariah, Mary and the suitors are seen.

Η ΠΡΟC ΤΟΝ ΙΩCΗΦ ΠΗΓΙΑΔΟCΙC

In the dome, the medallion of Mary is surrounded by 16 king prophets who are her ancestors. In the picture, Joram, Ozias and Joatham can be seen

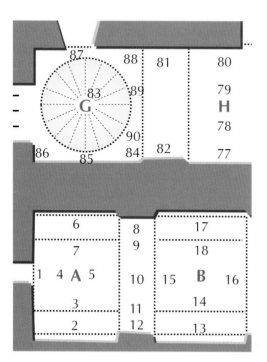

Genealogy of Mary

The inner surface of the northern dome in the inner narthex is decorated with mosaics representing the ancestors of Mary, surrounding the medallion in which Virgin and Christ child are depicted. These are David and the kings of the house of David: David, Solomon, Roboam, Abia, Asa, Josaphat, Joram, Ozias, Joatham, Achaz, Ezekias, Manasses, Amon, Josias, Jechonias, Salathiel. The figures of the lower zone do not belong to the ancestry of Christ. However, included in this group are depictions of Hananiah, Azariah, Mishael Daniel, Joshua, Moses, Aaron, Hur, Samuel, Job and Melchizedek. At two sides of Mary's head in the medallion are monograms of her name and abbreviations of her title 'Mother of God'.

In one of the pendentives of the dome is the scene of Joachim praying on the mountain (G-88). Joachim, the father of Mary, is shown grieving as he had no child. Seated on the mountain with shame, Joachim is pouring out his trouble to the young shepherds carrying sacks on their backs.

In the opposite pendentive is the scene of annunciation of the birth of Jesus Christ to Mary. Mary stands next to a well and Gabriel appears to her, breaking the news of the coming birth of Jesus.

Joachim praying with shepherd in the mountains
'Mary's Genealogy' in the dome

Birth of the Virgin

On the wall of the second bay in the inner narthex on the left is the scene of the birth of Mary. In front of the door, a young woman is seated on a stool, holding the infant Mary in her hands as another woman prepares the bath. Joachim peers out solicitously from the doorway. Three women in the back are busy with other things. A maid is helping Anne who is lying in the bed.

Joachim and Anne who were both descendants of David, had no child. On a feast day, when Joachim went to a temple to make a sacrifice, he was driven away by the priest since he had no child. Deeply saddened for this, Joachim ascended up into the mountains and passed his days with his shepherds. He stayed up there for 40 consecutive days and nights, praying and fasting. On the final day of the feast, Gabriel visited Anne to give her the news that she would be expecting a child soon, and meeting her husband at the Golden Gate of Jerusalem. Unaware of this, Joachim offered a sacrifice to God on the mountains. Anne then meeted Joachim at the Golden Gate as Gabriel had foretold and this elderly couple later had a girl named Mary.

The scene of 'the meeting of Anne and Joachim at the Golden Gate' (G-H 81)

'Birth of the Virgin' scene

ΗΓΕΝΝΗCΙCΤΗCΘΚΥ

Joseph Taking Leave of Mary

Joseph, with one of his sons, speaks the words of farewell to Mary. Standing in the middle before the big houses, a nimbed figure of Joseph is depicted as he raises his right hand in a gesture of greeting and walks away. Mary, her head bent over and her hands crossed in front of her at the waist, appears to be greatly troubled. The son of Joseph, carrying a basket, watches the scene. Next to this scene, in the corner designated as No. 86, one can see the Head Priest Zachariah rejecting the offers of Joachim to the temple. Unfortunately, the complementary mosaics of this composition are destroyed. On the adjacent mosaic designated as No. 87, the scene of the annunciation to Anne is shown. Gabriel appears to her as she stands in the middle of the garden near a fountain. A maid is watching them. In the transverse arch between the bays G and H are the scenes of the meeting of Joachim and Anne (G-H 81) and Joseph taking Virgin Mary to his house (G-H 82). Joseph standing in the front, looks back over his shoulder at Mary who is depicted as an innocent-looking young girl. One of the sons of Joseph is also seen in this scene.

Joseph taking Mary to his house (H-G 82)
The scene of 'Joseph taking leave of Mary'

The Death
of the Virgin

The scene of Mary's death is found on the inside of the gate that passes into the naos of the church. Mary is seen at rest in a catafalque. There are Apostles, clergymen, and soothsayers on both sides of her. One of the Apostles swings a censer, the others bend forward. Behind the bed, within the aureole stands Christ at the center of the panel. Christ holds in his hands a newborn infant representing the soul of Mary. Within the outer aureole stand the angels, and two cherubims hover in the upper part of the scene . One sees that the scene, including the facial expressions, curves in garments worn, and people's stances, were depicted in a fine and realistic manner.

On the right, on the front side of the abscissa pillar in the naos of the church, one sees Mary holding Jesus in her lap (93). Framed like an icon, this mosaic is partially destroyed. The inscription here reads "Chora Tor achoretou" meaning 'the dwelling place of the uncontainable'. A mosaic of Jesus is found on the north wall of the abscissa pillar. Although, the mosaic is in a very ruinous state, one can still make out Jesus holding in his hand the Gospels in which are written the words "Come unto me, al ye that labor and are heavy laden, and I will give you rest."

The scene of 'the dormition of the Virgin' above the entrance gate
to the main bay

The mosaic of Mary and the Christ child designated as 93 in the
main bay

Paracclesion

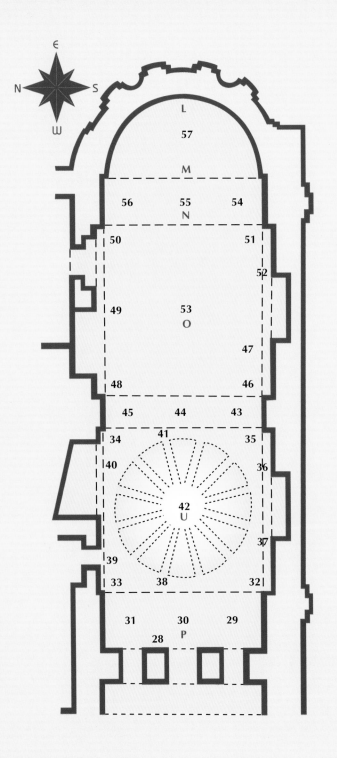

Plan of the Lower Zone

1. *Unidentified bust*
2. *St. Sabas Startelates*
3. *St. Procopius*
4. *St. Mercurius*
5. *St. David*
6. *St. Eustahius*
7. *St. Samonas*
8. *St. Gurias*
9. *St. Theodore Startelates*
10. *St. Theodore Tiro*
11. *St. Demetrius*
12. *St. Artemius or St. Nicetas*
13. *Medallion of Bacchus*
14. *Medallion of St. Sergius*
15. *Medallion of St. Lazarus*
16. *Medallion of St. Flarus*
17. *Unidentified saint*
18. *Medallion of an unidentified saint*
19. *Medallion of an unidentified saint*
20. *A saint in solitude (St. George?)*
21. *Virgin Eleousa*
22. *Unidentified church father*
23. *St. Athanasius*
24. *St. John Chrysostom*
25. *St. Basil*
26. *St. Gregory*
27. *St. Cyril of Alexandria*

Plan of the Upper Zone

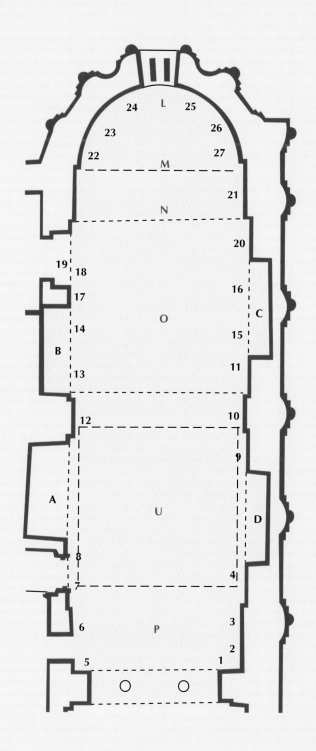

𝒫aracclesion

One reaches the Paracclesion or the cemetery chapel which was annexed by Theodor Metochites, by passing between two narrow columns. This chapel stretches the length of the churh and ends with a wide arched apse. Paracclesion attached to the south side of the nave, was built both for compensating the slope of the ground and serving as the mortuary chapel of the church. It was erected on a basement which was formerly used as crypt and then as a cistern. This basement is divided into two corridors. The length of the Paracclesion is 29 meters. It is composed of two square bays separated from each other by transverse arches and an apse. The first bay is covered by a dome raised on a drum containing windows, whereas the other is covered by a vault. The apse is half-circular from inside and in the shape of a polygon from the outside. Let us now, start to trace the frescoes of Paracclesion.

The Angel Smiting the Assyrians (No.29)

After passing between the columns, in the southern soffit of the western arch of the chapel is a scene illustrating the angel smiting the Assyrians. As the fulfillment of Isaiah's prophecy, the soldiers of Sennacherib, King of Assyrians, would not enter the city of Jerusalem and be smitten by an angel. Isaiah is seen on the left with the angel, holding an inscribed scroll. The inscription in his hand reads "And it came to pass at night that the angel of the Lord went forth, and smote in the camp of the Assyrians". In the pediment of

the gate between Isaiah's hand and the angel is a figure of Mary. And below are the depictions of St. Sabas Stratelates and St. Procopius on the wall (No. 2-3).

Impressive looks of the Anastasis and the Last Judgment frescoes in the vault of the Paracclesion

Generic view of the Paracclesion

Blessed Souls (No.30)

In the middle of this section, on top of the western arch is the remaining painting of the blessed souls in the hand of God. This composition is attributed to Solomon's verses in his Book of Wisdom, which reads "The souls of the righteous are in the hand of God and tortures of death shall not touch them". In the composition, a hand which holds within it infants wrapped in swaddling cloths representing the souls of the righteous, is seen. The two figures below must be of David's and Soloman's.

The Virgin, Child Jesus and Angels (No. 42)

In the dome of the second bay the 'Mother of God' in the center and the Christ Child on her lap and the angels surrounding her are painted. The dome was divided into twelve pieces by twelve windows which provide proper light to the figure of Mary in the dome. Above these windows are the frescoes of twelve angels holding spears. Four of them are holding a sphere symbolizing the earth. These are Archangel Michael, Uriel, Rafael, and Gabriel. The Virgin is pictured as the Queen of the Heaven while holding the Christ Child clad in golden garments and making a sign of blessing. The angels are clothed brilliantly colored attires of the Byzantium Palace. The decorations of the ribs that separate the angel figures are ornamented with various plant or flower forms.

The Pictures of the Hymnographers (No. 32-33)

In the pendentives below the dome, four hymnographers are portrayed in the act of composition. These poets were writing their hymns to honor Virgin Mary. In the southwestern pendentive, a 9th century hymnographer, St. Joseph the Poet, is pictured as he holds a scroll that he has

Two views of frescoes of the apse in the Paracclesion

written. In the background, the scenes are related to the stories of the Old Testament.

In the northwestern pendentive (No. 33) is again a 9th century hymnographer, Theophanes Graptos, so called because he was branded on the face during the iconoclastic persecutions. He is depicted as he writes lines for a funeral. Also, he served as a monk in the Chora Monastery in which he was buried after he died.

Tomb D

Centered in the south wall is the tomb of Michael Tornikes who was a close friend of Metochites. Tornikes was a Grand Constable in the Palace, but he lost his rank after the coup of 1328, and was buried here after his death.

From the epitaph above his tomb, we learn that Tornikes was of royal lineage, held high ranks in the imperial court and successfully became Grand Constable. Here, also fragmented figures of Christ and Archangel can be seen. The survived part of the decoration today consists of mosaics and frescoes that portray Mary and Christ Child at the center and Tornikes and his wife at either side. At the base level of the arch are the portraits of the Monk Makarios and the Nun Eugenia.

Jacob Wrestling with the Angel (No. 39)

Opposite to the tomb D are two scenes of Jacob who saw God in his dream. One of these scenes which were taken from the Old Testament, depicts Jacob as he wrestles with the angel. He starts to wrestle with the angel as he sees God face to face. Jacob is seen beardless. The scene above this shows Jacob's vision of the ladder that reaches to heaven, on which angels ascend and descend and above which stands the Lord. Jacob's ladder is seen rising in a curve to parallel the contour of the vault.

Jacob, son of Issac received his father's blessing to become

a rightful heir and patriarch of the tribe instead of his older twin Esau. Esau was very angry and started to make plans to kill him. To save his life, his mother Rebekah sent him to find shelter in Haran, with her brother Lavan. He set out on a long journey to Haran. One night, he put a stone under his head as a pillow and slept. He saw a ladder in his dream leading up to heaven, with angels ascending and descending. God told him "I am the God of Abraham, your father, and of Isaac," and continued "I will give the land where you lie to you and to your seed. You shall spread abroad to the east and to the north and to the south. In you and in your seed shall all the families of the earth be blessed. I am with you and wherever you go, I will protect you and bring you back to this land." Jacob awakened and thought "God is here, but I couldn't notice." Then he erected the stone he had used as a pillow as a monument and called it Bethel. There he made a vow to God. This is the story of Jacob's ladder in the Old Testament. The story of Jacob wrestling with the angel is as follows.

After 20 years, to make peace with his brother Esau, Jacob left Haran with his two wives and eleven sons. He sent all his belongings, his wives and sons across the river Jabbok. He remained on the other side. Darkness fell. There he started to wrestle with a stranger in his dream and continued until the day broke. Finally, the stranger spoke "Let me go, for the day breaks." Then Jacob understanding that he was an angel, said firmly, "I will not let you go unless you bless me." Then the man asked his name and he replied "Jacob". "Your name shall no more be called Jacob but Israel," the voice said. "For as a prince you have power with God and with men and have prevailed." And he

The fresco of soldier and saint Theologos

Tomb D. The portraits of Michael Tornikes and of his wife to whom the tomb belongs

blessed him. Jacob called the place Penuel and left. While wrestling with the angel, the hollow of Jacob's thigh was out of joint, therefore Israelis do not eat the sinew which is on the hollow of the thigh even today.

John of Damascus (No. 34)

In the northeastern pendentive of the dome is another hymnographer; John of Damascus who lived in the 8th century and who was a theologian and one of the most famous poets of his time. Popular by his distinguished turban, he wrote 'Idiomela for the Funeral Service".

Moses and The Burning Bush (No. 40)

In the lower zones of the northeastern pendentive, next to the window are scenes of appearance of God to Moses. In the scene in the arch, God appears to Moses in front of the burning bush and Moses has taken out his shoes, because the ground on which he stands is holy. In the third scene in the adjoining arch, Moses who is afraid of looking at God is hiding his face. Here, the burning bush signifies the Virgin Birth. For as the bush burned but was not consumed, so Mary conceived and gave birth but remained virgin.

Tomb of Theodore Metochites, Tomb A

The tomb in the northwestern wall of the Paracclesion is the one in which Theodore Methochites was buried (A). As mentioned in the previous chapters, Metochites served the Palace for years and promoted up to the second highest position after the emperor. Then he lost his power and was sent to exile. Later, he was forgiven and returned to the church which he had once repaired and decorated with the magnificent mosaics and frescoes. He lived here as a

The fresco of soldier St. George

Soldier and St. Procopius and St. Sabas Stratelates

destitute monk and was buried in here after he died. The tomb of Metochites, however, lost all its ornamentations. During the Ottoman period the wall here, was removed for opening a passageway between the naos and this bay and therefore the sculptured busts of Christ and archangels could partially survived to the present day.

Solomon and the Israelites (No.36)

In the southeastern pendentive, Cosmas the poet, the student of John of Damascus is shown with his uninscribed codex on his lap(No.35). In the adjoining arch, Solomon and the Israelites can be seen. Solomon, son of David, was a king and a prophet like his father. According to the Bible, he is the King of Israel and according to the Koran he is a prophet of the Jews and a king as well. Solomon after succeeding to the throne of Israel as a very young king was confused and prayed to God. God appeared to him in a dream and said "Ask what I shall give you." And Solomon asked for an understanding heart to judge the people, to discern between good and bad. Pleased by his requests God gave him a wise and understanding heart and also other skills that he did not ask for. For example he could command the animals and speak with birds.

Solomon here is shown as he wears the vestments of a Byzantine emperor, with a slender staff and a holy book and leading the elders of Israel. There are figures of rock and tree in the background.

Priests Carrying the Sacred Vessels (No.43)

In the arch next to the domed section is the scene of priests carrying the sacred vessels to Solomon's temple. One of them is bearing the seven-branched candlestick symbolizing Mary, while the other is carrying a large bowl in which the divine food was kept.

There are medallions of standing portraits of the martyr-saints on the wall as saviors of the deceased and guards of the tombs.

St. Theodoros is on the southern wall next to the founder's tomb. St. Sabas Stratelates and soldier St. Procopius are on the wall of the Paracclesion. Depictions of some of the saints of the monastery are placed on the west side of the south wall. On the northwestern corner, St. David from Thessalonica who spent 3 years of his life on a tree top, can be seen. Next to the eastern gate is a fragmented picture of another saint.

Melchizedek (No. 38)

In the crowns of the arches are four medallion portraits. Below the dome cornice, depictions of Jesus and Melchizedek, the King of Salem, can be seen. Melchizedek the Righteous, greeted Abraham when he returned from a battle and offered bread and wine to him and blessed him.

Michael (No. 55)

In the arch in the center of the soffit is another medallion of a portrait of Jesus, but it is mostly destroyed. Medallion of Archangel Michael is placed in the eastern vault. It is believed that Michael serves as the conductor of souls to judgment and the righteous to heaven. Therefore, he must have been placed near the Last Judgment scene. Theodore Metochites had written a plea for him to be the Savior of his soul.

Medallion portraits, Last Judgment scene and figures in mandorlas (the aureole in an almond-like shape, surrounding the figures of the holy people) as well as the painting of the sky along side the vaults of the chapel form a unity in a composition like that of an enormous icon.

Tombs B and C

Now let us pass to the second bay of the Paracclesion, in order to see the frescoes in the dome. Before entering to the second bay, one can see two tombs placed opposite to each other. Almost all of the decoration of the tomb in the northern wall is destroyed. Above the niche are the rosettes of the saints Sergius and Bacchus. The decoration of the tomb that is designated as C in our plan is still relatively intact. The personages portrayed here are not known. The painting style is quite different, inferior than the others. There are four figures on the back wall. The couple in the middle is dressed in princely costumes: man with the cape and woman with the crown. Her dress is decorated with the monograms of Palailogos and Asanes families. At the far left

is a woman in a plain dress and at the far right is a nun. All the faces were restored during the Byzantium period. In the arch of the niche, on the marble decoration are the depictions of Jesus and archangel.

In the pendentive at the northwest, an angel and a soul are painted (No. 48). The angel is presenting the soul for judgment. This scene is believed to depict the Archangel Michael presenting the soul of Metochites for the final judgment. Also, it is claimed by others that this soul belongs to Lazarus the beggar.

As we proceed along the north wall, the scene of entry of the elect into Heaven (No. 49) can be seen in the northern arch of the eastern section. This is the final element in the composition of the Last Judgment. The gate of the Heaven guarded by a cherub divides the scene into two equal parts. To the left, St. Peter who is trying to open the gate with a key leads the crowd of the Elect which consists of bishops, martyrs, holy monks. To the right, a white luxuriant garden filled with plants represents the heaven. The figure of the Good Thief clad in a loincloth, holds a wooden cross, greets the Elect and gestures toward the Virgin attended by two angels.

Abraham and Lazarus the Beggar (No.50)

The painting in the northeastern pendentive represents Abraham with Lazarus the Beggar at his bosom, surrounded with the group of souls of the blessed. Abraham is seated on a throne in the midst of green plants and holds Lazarus the beggar, represented as a child, with his right hand. In the background is the portray of Heaven.

Abraham is of lineage of Shem, son of Noah. Terah was the father of Abraham, Nahor and Haran who was the father of

Mary and the Christ child figure in the dome and the 12 attending angels around.

Lot. Abraham and his wife Sarah had no child. Sarah let him to have a child from a maidservant in order for Abraham to have an heir. And Ishmael was born. Later, miraculously, his wife Sarah bore him a son when he was 100 years old, and Isaac was born. Then God put him to a test of his faith and ordered him to take Isaac to the mountains and sacrifice him. But at the last moment, God sent him a ram to sacrifice and saved Isaac.

On the eastern axis of the vault, next to the figure of Christ in Judgment are the scenes of the empty throne of the Etimasia and the weighing of the souls. In the Orthodox tradition, Etimasia is the empty throne which is prepared for the second coming of Jesus. The Book of the Gospels and a double-armed cross are placed on it. The source of this theme is from the Book of the Gospels in which is written "Justice and judgment are the habitations of thy throne". In front of the throne, at either side are Adam and Eve in attitudes of proskynesis. Below the throne of Etimasia is the scene in which the records of the souls are weighed in the scale. The souls are shown as nude infants and the records as bundles of scrolls. At the center stands a single soul trembling and awaiting judgment. At the right is a painting of a black devil in a highly deteriorated state, attempting to pull the scale on his side downward. But the souls are on their way to Heaven on the right, while the little devils lead the captive souls into hell.

The Last Judgment (No. 53)

In the domical vault, in the middle of this bay is the scene of the Last Judgment. After the splendid Anastasis fresco in the apse, this scene is one of the most crowded scenes in the

Generic look of the frescoes in the Paracclesion

The fresco of 'the angel carrying the universe' above 'the Last Judgment' fresco. The universe is depicted as a roll here.

Byzantine Art. At the very center of the panel Christ seated on a throne within the mandorla, occupies the most prominent position in the composition. His open right hand making a gesture of acceptance to the Elect who approach, is held higher than his left hand which is making a rejection to the cursed souls in hell. The Virgin on the left, and John the Baptist on the right are pictured as intercessors on behalf of mankind. Also, the twelve Apostles are seated on the benches at each side of Jesus as they are holding open books, so that a scene called 'Deesis' in the Byzantine Art is created. Behind the Apostles and Jesus, the attendant angels stand in groups, filling the entire width of the composition.

Above these, just at the center of the vault, is an angel in full flight carrying a snail, representing the paradise. This is the first time in the Byzantine Art that a snail representing the paradise, is pictured. This spiral figure illustrates the scroll being unfurled and then rolled together.

Above the four clouds that form a half circle around the northeast and southwest zones of the vault, are choirs of the Elect. These are bishops, holy women and men, martyrs, Apostles and prophets. Some of them kneel on the cloud and pray. The choir of bishops is composed of twenty four figures with vestments on which are red or black crosses. The Apostles are wearing monk suits. Prophets are dressed in usual himations, David and Solomon are leading the group.

The Land and Sea Giving Up Their Dead (No. 46)

In the southwestern pendentive of the domical vault is the scene of the two angels blowing trumpets as the land and sea give up their dead. The clusters of dead upon hearing the sound, are being resurrected.

'The Last Judgment' fresco in Paracclesion

Aaron and His Sons (No. 31)

Three priests are seen before the altar. These are High Priest Aaron and his sons. The theme is related to their burnt offering on the altar upon a dream of Hezekiah.

Bringing the Ark of The Covenant (No. 47)

In the southern lunette of the second arch are the episodes of bringing the Ark of the Covenant to the temple. The Ark is depicted as a gabled structure with sloping top, covered with a purple cloth. Before the construction of Solomon's temple, the Ark was in Sion, known also as the city of David. Solomon gathers the elders of Israel to bring the Ark of the Covenant to Jerusalem. The Old Testament or Torah is the holy book of the Jews. It includes Solomon's The Book of Proverbs which consists of thirty one chapters and The Song of Solomon which consists of eight chapters. The bearers of the Ark appear to walk toward the right. In the background Sion can be seen through the rocky mountains.

The making of the Ark of the Covenant is described in the Old Testament as follows:

"And they shall make an ark of shittim wood; 2 cubits and a half shall be the length thereof, and a cubit and a half shall be the width and height.

And you shall overlay it with pure gold, within and without you shall overlay it, and shall make upon it a crown of gold roundabout. And you shall cast four rings of gold for it and put them in the four corners thereof, and two rings shall be in one side of it and two rings in the other side of it. And you shall make staves of shittim wood, and overlay them with gold. And you shall put the staves into the rings by the sides

Fresco of the hymnographer Cosmas in the lower part of the dome in which there is the fresco of the Virgin

Abraham and Lazarus the Beggar at his bosom

of the ark and the ark may be borne with them.

And you shall put in the ark the testimony which I shall give you. And you shall make a mercy seat of pure gold. And you shall make two cherubims of gold of beaten work, in the two ends of the mercy seat. And you shall put the mercy seat above the ark and in the ark you shall put the testimony that I shall give you.

And there I will meet you, I will commune with you from above the mercy seat between the two cherubims which are upon the ark of the testimony, of all things which I will give you in commandment unto the children of Israel" (Exodus 25:10-23)

The Ark was in the tabernacle where the Israelites used to worship and then it was placed in the holiest corner in the

The scene of Christ Raising the Daughter of Jarius

temple. Apart from the tablets, some other sacred things were also kept in the ark.

The Rich Man in Hell (No. 51)

In the southeastern pendentive is the scene of the rich man in Hell. Before his death, this man was living in luxury, wearing purple garments of linen and enjoying the life in richness. One day, a wounded beggar called Lazarus was left at his door. Lazarus was trying to survive with his daily residuals. Then the poor man died.

The angels took him next to Abraham. Shortly after, the rich man died, too. The rich man is seen as he suffers amidst the flames of Hell. Below him are two moneybags and, spilled out at his feet are a large number of golden coins. While the

The Righteous entering Heaven, are lead by St Peter. Figures of an angel, a good thief holding a cross at the gate of Heaven and Mary among the angels in Heaven.

141

flames are surrounding him, he turns to the left to face Abraham at the opposite side of the arch of the bema, as he beseeches him to send Lazarus "that he may dip the tip of his finger in water, and cool my tongue". Abraham replies "between us and you there is a great gulf fixed: so that they which would pass from hence to you cannot; neither can they pass to us, that would come thence" (Luke 16:19-26)

Above this scene is the image of the fiery stream and the lake of fire. The Lake of Fire flows down from the left foot of Christ to the southeastern pendentive. Although it is highly deteriorated, the faces of the suffering souls can be determined. Some of them are shown in princely costumes and some wear wide hats like of Metochites'.

The Torments of the Damned (No. 52)

In the south wall, the torments of the damned are depicted. These are next to the figure of the Rich Man in Hell, in the

The Last Judgment' fresco in Paracclesion

pendentive in the eastern side of the arch. There are four monochromatic paintings showing the damned suffering the torments of Hell. On the wall in the lower zone is the figure of St. George (?) with his sword and spear in his hand (No. 20).

The Virgin Eleousa (No. 21)

In the lower part of the wall on the right of the apse, is the figure of the Virgin Eleousa. This type of description

showing Mary as the 'Merciful' or 'Compassionate' is known as 'Eleousa'. Mary holds the infant Jesus and presses her cheek against his son's with tenderness. The candles burned here caused the fresco to fade and the figure of Christ next to this scene has been completely lost.

The Raising of the Daughter of Jarius (No. 54)

In the both sides of the arch of the apse are two miraculous scenes of Jesus. They complete the Anastasis fresco in the

An impressive look of the Anastasis fresco.

Next page: 'The church fathers' below the Anastasis fresco. These are from left to right St. Basile, St. Gregory, and St. Cyril.

143

Ο ΑΓ[ΙΟС]

ΒΑСΙ
ΛΕ
ΟС

Ο ΑΓΙΟС
ΓΡΗΓΟ
ΡΙΟС

Ο ΘΕΟΛΟ/ΓΟ/Σ   ΚΥΡΙΛΛΟ/Σ

apse. In the southern side of the arch is the scene of the raising of the daughter of Jarius. The dead is seen lying in the bed, in the house. Jesus grasping the wrist of the maiden resurrects her. The daughter of Jarius, restored to life, sits upright on her bed. The Apostles and the parents amazed, are witnessing the miracle.

The Raising of the Widow's Son (No. 56)

In the north side of the arch of the apse is the scene of the resurrection of the son of a widow. One day Jesus went to a city called Nain with many of his disciples. When he came near the gate of the city, he saw a dead man carried out, the only son of a widow, and had compassion for her and said "Weep not". He touched the bier and said "Young man, I say unto you, Arise" Then he sat up and began to speak. (Luke 7: 11-15)

The Anastasis Fresco (No. 57)

The composition in the semi-dome of the apse is the 'Anastasis' fresco. In the eastern Christian art, the scene of Jesus' descent to Hell is called 'Anastasis'. Depicted here symbolically is his triumph over death and his redemption of the Righteous of the old dispensation. In this splendid fresco of Anastasis, Christ in his white garments, standing between the two, simultaneously raises Adam with his right hand and Eve with his left, from their sarcophagi.

Christ is depicted in a very strong manner within the mandorla with the hues of light blue along its outer contour and in which the stars are scattered. The Apostles appear in each side of Christ in two groups. On the left are also the prophets David and Solomon pointing him with their hands, and John the Baptist.

The Virgin Eleousa pictured with the infant Jesus at her bosom in the apse of the Paracclesion

The clustered people behind the Virgin to the right of the Anastasis fresco. Abel is seen in the front with his crook.

The figures on the left of the Anastasis fresco. Here John the Baptist is seen in the front, together with the prophets David and Solomon

To the right of the panel, behind Eve, apart from the clustered people is Abel wearing a green tunic as he holds his shepherd's crook. Beneath the feet of Christ are the broken gates of Hell and shackled figure of Satan.

Below the Anastasis fresco are six church fathers (No. 22-27). All of them are dressed in bishops' vestments. The first figure on the left is partially destroyed and since its inscription is also lost, it cannot be identified. The others from left to right are: St. Athanasius, St. John Chrysostom, St. Basil. St. Gregory the Theologian, and St. Cyril of Alexandria.

Let us here give brief information on them:

1. St. Atahnasius: He was a theologian who was born in Alexandria around 295 and died in 373 in the same city. He was also the Bishop of Alexandria and attended the Great Consul which was held in Iznik (Nicaea) in 325. He was a keen advocate of Orthodoxy against Arianism and devoted to the divinity of Jesus Christ. He was sent to exile a few times because of his thoughts. In all his books there are discussions against Arianism.

2. St John Chrysostom: He was born in Antioch in a rich family between the years 340 and 350. He was a Christian moralist and a saint. He was sent to the best schools, took lectures from famous Libanius and Diodorus of Tarsus. He became priest in 386. He acquired popularity with his stirring speeches and was called to Istanbul and became the Bishop of Constantinople. Because of his fierce criticisms of the Empress Eudoxia and of the Bishop of Alexandria, he was sent to exile to Anatolia by the verdict of a synod which

was held in 403. But by the threats of the excited people who loved Chrysostom, the Emperor Arsacius recalled him. Chrysostom who had taken his position back, complained against a silver statue of Eudoxia in the square just before Hagia Sofia, and was deposed by the Emperor again in 404. He was sent to exile in Cappadocia first, then in Comanon in Pontus and died there in 407.

3. St. Basil: He was born in Kayseri in Cappadocia and died in 379 at the same place. He was educated in Istanbul, then went to Athens and returned to Kayseri. He became a priest in 362 and was elected as the Bishop of Kayseri in 370. He took part in the religion wars in the Near East. He was strictly against Arianism and wrote a lot of books of which The Rules of St. Basileius is famous.

4. St. Gregory: He was from Cappadocia. He lived between the years 330 and 390. He was educated in Kayseri, Alexandria and Athens. In 372 he became the bishop of Sasima and then Nazianzus. He was appointed as the bishop of Constantinople with the mission of establishing Orthodoxy against Arianism. He was deposed by the decision of Istanbul Consul held in 381 and lived in solitude until his death.

5. St. Cyril: He was born in 376 in Alexandria and died in 444 at the same place. He became the Bishop of Alexandria in 412, attended Ephesus Consul in 431. He was a firm advocate of the Orthodoxy. He was deposed by Theodosius II, but later was recalled and took his position back. He led the Eastern Christians until his death.

Jesus in Anastasis fresco. Christ is depicted in white garments within the mandorla with hues of light blue and scattered stars

Next page: an impressive look of the Anastasis fresco. Here Jesus is shown descended to Hell to raise Adam and Eve from their sarcophagi

 Glossary

Aaron: The first high priest of Israelites. He joined to Moses against the pharaoh, was a commander and a spokesman of Moses.

Abel: Son of Adam who was killed by his brother Cain

Anastasis: In the Orthodox tradition, the scene of Jesus' descent to Hell

Apocrypha: The collective name of fourteen books not considered canonical, which are included in the Old Testament by the Roman Catholic Church but denied by the Protestant Churches

Apse: A portion of any building forming a termination or projection semicircular or polygonal in plan, and having a dome or vaulted roof.

Archesoleum: A tomb with an arch over it

Baptistery: A building or a portion of a building in which the rite of baptism is administered.

Basilica: A church, rectangular in shape, with a middle and two side aisles divided by columns, and an apse.

Bema: The enclosed space surrounding the altar; the sanctuary or chancel

Blachernitissa: One of the types of depictions of Mary in the Orthodox tradition. Usually, Mary is shown holding the infant Jesus in her bosom.

Catacomb: A subterranean burial place where the early Christian gather secretly from the Romans

Chapel: Small church for prayer and worship

Cherub: A winged celestial figure regarded as a guardian of a sacred place generally represented as winged children

Christogram: A monogram or a symbol symbolizing Christ

Ciborium: A permanent dome-shaped canopy placed over an altar

Daniel: A Jewish prophet who was sent to exile by Babylonian King Nebuchadnezzar in 597 B.C.

David: A prophet and the second King of Israel who lived between the years 1015 and 975 B.C.

Deesis: A scene that shows Christ , Mary and John the Baptist together which means praying

Diaconicon: Dressing room or a chapel placed to the north of the apse, in Byzantine churches

Eleousa: A type of description of Mary in the Orthodox tradition. Mary is shown while holding the infant Jesus with her arms and pressing her chin against her son's with tenderness

Etimasia: Empty throne prepared for the second coming of Jesus, on which are the Book of the Gospels and the double-armed cross.

Frescoe: A method of painting on a plastered wall or ceiling

Grek Cross: A cross consisting of an upright crossed in the middle by a horizontal piece of the same length. The plan of a church

Habakkuk: A prophet of Jews mentioned in the Old Testament (around 600 B.C.)

Herod: King of Judaea during the time of Jesus

Hipoje: An underground tomb

Hodagetria: A type of the description of Mary in the Orthodox tradition. She holds Christ in her left arm and raising her right hand in a gesture of supplication

Idiomela: Byzantine Hymns chanted to their own particular melody or meter

Icon: A religious image of Jesus, Mary or saints in the Christian churches or houses

Isaac Comnenos: Byzantine prince, son of Alexius I

Jacob: Son of Isaac and Rebekah; a king and a prophet of the Jews

John: One of the four writers of the Bible

Koimesis: The scene showing the death of the Virgin in the Orthodox tradition

Kontakion: A short poem to celebrate a feast or a saint

Liturgy: The ritual or established formulas for public worship

Logothete: High rank official in the palace

Luke: One of the four writers of the Bible

Mandorla: The aureole in the shape of an almond that surrounds the descriptions of holy personages

Mark: One of the four writers of the Bible

Martyry: A shrine built in tribute to a Christian martyr

Matthew: One of the four writers of the Bible

Melane: Byzantine Princess married to the Mongolian Prince Abaga Khan, and later returned to Istanbul upon the death of her husband and became a nun in the Chora Monastery

Monogram: A character consisting of two or more letters inscribed for decoration or identification of God, prophets or kings

Moses: Prophet who was the founder of Judaism. He lived in mid-13th century B.C.

Naos: The main section in the Orthodox churches where people worship

Narthex: A vestibule that lies between the principal entrance of a church and the nave

Nave: The middle part, lengthwise, of a church, often including a clerestory

Niche: Recess or hollow, as in a wall for a statue or other decorative object

Pantocrator: One of the titles of Christ which means "omnipotent"

Pendentive: A triangular, concave masonry device which provides a transition from a circular or polygonal plan as a dome to a supporting construction of another plan, as a rectangle

Paracclesion: A cemetery chapel annexed to a church in the Byzantine architecture

Pastophoria: The places on either side of the apse in Byzantine churches

Praetor: In ancient Rome, originally a title of consuls later belonging to the magistrates who administered the justice in the city

Proskynesis: Reverence in a prostrate attitude

Prothesis: The preparation of the Eucharistic elements in Orthodox churches, the table on which this is done, the part of bema or sanctuary where this table stands

Pulpit: A platform or raised structure in a church from which the clergyman delivers the sermon

Regalia: The ensigns or symbols of royalty in Byzantine era

Relic: A bone or other part of saints or martyrs, some parts of their garments, or the like, preserved and regarded with veneration

Salome: Niece and stepdaughter of Herod Antipas. She caused the beheading of John the Baptist by her dance

Solomon: Jewish king and a prophet who lived between 970 and 931 B.C.

Synthronon: Priest's bench, a piece of furniture that was commonly found against the curved wall of the apse of an early Christian church

Tessera: A small cube of marble used in mosaic work

- **TURKEY (Little Format)**
  (In Engilish, German, French)

- **ANCIENT CIVILISATIONS OF TURKEY (Large)**
  (In Engilish, Turkish)

- **ISTANBUL (Little Format)**
  (In Engilish, German, French, Italian, Spanish)

- **CAPITAL OF THREE EMPIRES ISTANBUL (Large)**
  (In Engilish, Turkish)

- **TOPKAPI PALACE (Little Format)**
  (In Engilish, German, French, Italian, Spanish)

- **TOPKAPI PALACE (Large Format)**
  (In Engilish, German, French)

- **PAMUKKALE - HIERAPOLIS**
  (In Engilish, German, French, Italian, Spanish, Swedish, Dutch, Japanese)

- **CAPPADOCIA**
  (In Engilish, German, French, Italian, Spanish)

- **EPHESUS, KUŞADASI, PRIENE, MILET, DIDYMA**
  (In Engilish, German, French)

- **LYCIA**
  (In Engilish, German, French, Turkish)

- **A BLUE ROMANCE (Large Format)**
  (In Engilish, Turkish)

- **ANTALYA**
  (In Engilish, German, French, Italian)

- **MEVLANA AND THE MEVLANA MUSEUM**
  (In Engilish, German, French)

- **CHORA**
  (In Engilish, German, French)

- **TURKISH CARPET ART**
  (In Engilish, German, French)

- **HAREM**
  (In Engilish, German, French, Turkish)

- **HAGIA SOPHIA**
  (In Engilish, German, French)

www. aksityayincilik.com

İlhan Akşit

İlhan Akşit was born in Denizli in 1940. He graduated as an archaeologist in 1965. When he was assigned to a post related to the excavation of Aphrodisias. He was director of the Çanakkale - Troy Museum between 1968-1976, during which time the replica of the Trojan horse we now see on the site was constructed.

He directed the excavation of the Chryse Apollo temple over a period of five years. From 1976-1978, the author acted as director of the Underwater Archaeology Museum, Bodrum and was appointed Director of National Palaces in 1978. During his directorship, the author was responsible for the restoration and reopening of these palaces to the public after an extended period of closure.

1982 he retired from his post to take up a career as an author of popular books on Turkish archaeology and tourism. He has nearly 30 titles to his credit to date, including "The Story of Troy", "Chora", The Civilizations of Anatolia", "İstanbul", The Blue Sailing", "The Hittites", "Cappadocia", "The Topkapı Palace", "Pamukkale", "Mustafa Kemal Atatürk", "Antalya", "Ephesus", "Lycia", "Harem" and "Turkey"